Logo for the Macintosh®

An Introduction Through Object Logo™

by Harold Abelson and Amanda Abelson

Paradigm Software Incorporated
Cambridge, Massachusetts

This book is published by
Paradigm Software Incorporated
P.O. Box 2995
Cambridge, MA 02238
U.S.A.
(617) 576-7675

The book was set in Times Roman and Helvetica by Rebecca Bisbee,
Boston, and was printed and bound by ZBR Publications in the
United States of America.

Managing Editor: Hazem Sayed
Project Editors: Katherine Fong and Mohammed Zaidi
Cover Design: Mitchell Zweibel. Dedicated to Bernice, Andrea and
Harmony.

Object Logo: Steve Hain

Library of Congress catalog card number: 92-62694

ISBN 1-882527-03-8

 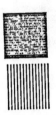

MIT Press
0262510693
ABELSON
OBJ LOGO BK

for Lynn (Mom)

Table of Contents

vii

viii

Introduction

Logo is the name for a philosophy of education and for a continually evolving family of computer languages that aid its realization. Its learning environments articulate the principle that giving people personal control over powerful computational resources can enable them to establish intimate contact with profound ideas from science, from mathematics, and from the art of intellectual model building. Its computer languages are designed to transform computers into flexible tools to aid in learning, in playing, and in exploring.

Logo was initially created in 1968 as part of a National Science Foundation sponsored research project conducted at Bolt, Beranek & Newman, Inc., in Cambridge, Massachusetts (Feurzeig, *et. al.* [10]). Throughout the 1970s the majority of Logo development was conducted at MIT in the Artificial Intelligence Laboratory and the Division for Study and Research in Education, using large research computer systems. By the end of the decade, personal computers capable of supporting Logo had become inexpensive enough for use in homes and schools. The first Logo implementations for personal computers, developed at MIT, were for the Texas Instruments and the Apple home computers.[1] These were followed by Logo systems for most of the personal computers that have since appeared. Logo assumed, and retains, a major role in educational computing at all levels, from elementary school through college.

Logo's designers were guided by the vision of an educational tool with no threshold and no ceiling. They were trying to make it possible for even young children to control the computer in self-directed ways, even at their first exposure to Logo. At the same time, they believed that Logo should be a general-purpose programming system of considerable power and wealth of expression. In fact, these two goals were complementary rather than conflicting, since it is the very lack of expressive power of primitive languages such as BASIC that makes it difficult for beginners to write simple programs that do interesting things. People of all backgrounds and abilities enjoy using Logo to create original and sophisticated programs. Logo has been successfully and productively used by preschool, elementary, junior high, high school, and college students, and by their teachers.

Some of the important features of Logo are

[1] The TI Logo implementation was carried out under the supervision of Seymour Papert. Principal contributors to this effort were Gary Drescher, Edward Hardebeck, Mark Gross, Leigh Klotz, and John Berlow. The Apple implementation was carried out under the supervision of Hal Abelson, by Steve Hain, Leigh Klotz, and Patrick Sobalvarro. Both systems benefited significantly from comments by Andy diSessa and Dan Watt.

- Logo is a *procedural* language. Logo programs are created by combining commands into groups called procedures, and using these procedures as steps in other procedures, and so on to arbitrary levels of complexity. Each individual step of a procedure may be any primitive Logo command or any user-defined procedure. Procedures can communicate among themselves via *inputs* and *outputs*.

- Logo is an *interactive* programming language. Any Logo command, whether built into the language or defined as a procedure, can be evaluated by simply typing the command at the keyboard.

- Logo's data objects (those things that can be named by individual variables, passed directly as inputs to procedures, and returned as values) include not only numbers and character strings, but also compound structures called *lists*. Many computer languages force the programmer to manipulate data structures in terms of sequences of operations on individual numbers and character strings. In contrast, Logo's lists are functional units that can be transformed in single operations, and this makes Logo a convenient and powerful language for applications involving symbol manipulation. Moreover, the fact that Logo procedures can themselves be represented and manipulated as lists means that users can attain considerable direct control over the way that commands are interpreted, for example, to provide special interfaces to Logo for the physically handicapped or the very young.[2]

Another important aspect of Logo is its incorporation of a programming area called *turtle geometry*. A turtle is a computer-controlled "cybernetic animal" that lives on the display screen and responds to Logo commands that make it move (**FORWARD** or **BACK**) and rotate (**LEFT** or **RIGHT**). As the turtle moves, it leaves a trace of its path, and in this way can be used to make drawings on the display screen. For example, the following Logo procedure tells Logo how to make the turtle draw a square by repeating four times the commands "go **FORWARD** 100 units, turn **RIGHT** 90 degrees":

```
TO SQUARE
REPEAT 4 [FORWARD 100 RIGHT 90]
END
```

In this book, we use turtle graphics to introduce the basic ideas of Logo programming, although we also cover other aspects of the

---

[2] Section 8.2 gives an example of a such an interface. The implementation makes use of the fact that it is possible to write Logo procedures that themselves define procedures. The books by Goldenberg [12] and Weir [30] describe work using Logo with physically and emotionally handicapped children.

language.[3]

Object Logo

Object Logo for the Apple Macintosh has been under development since 1986. Object Logo includes all the features found in other Logo systems, but it goes beyond them in incorporating *object-oriented programming*. Object-oriented programming was initially invented in the 1960s, in languages for programming computer simulations. But over the past few years, it has become exceedingly popular in the professional programming community as a general and flexible methodology for handling all sorts of programming tasks. Object-oriented programming, together with Object Logo's wide repertoire of commands for harnessing the capabilities of the Apple Macintosh, make Object Logo the most powerful version of Logo available today.

A guide to this book

The original edition of this book, based on the first Logo implementations for personal computers, was published in 1982. This new edition has been updated and revised to form an introduction to Logo programming based on Object Logo running on the Macintosh, although it can also be used with other versions of Logo. In general, we use "Logo" when referring to features common to most Logo systems, and "Object Logo" when discussing features specific to Object Logo. If you are using this book with another version of Logo, you will need to refer to the documentation for that system for specifics on loading, running, and using that version.

You should think about learning Logo in three stages. The first stage, covered in chapters 1 and 2, includes the basics of defining procedures and using turtle graphics to draw pictures on the display screen. Chapter 3 consists of suggestions for programming projects based on this material. Chapter 4 describes the mechanics of keeping track of procedures and saving them in files. The next stage in learning Logo includes writing procedures that use "data"—numbers, words, and lists, as introduced in chapter 5—to carry out projects such as the ones presented in chapter 6. Chapter 7 introduces object-oriented programming. Chapter 8 describes some more complex Logo programs, with an emphasis on programs that are interactive. Chapters 9 and 10 cover advanced topics in Logo programming, including using recursion to deal with words and lists, and using lists to represent complex data structures. Chapter 11 is a reference that describes the most commonly used primitive commands included in the Object Logo system.

---

[3] In his book *Mindstorms* [21], Papert discusses the turtle as exemplary of the kind of computational "object to think with" through which technology can lead to fundamental educational change. *Mindstorms* also discusses the Logo philosophy of education and the role of computer technology in transforming education. The book by Abelson and diSessa [1] uses turtle geometry as the basis for exploring in mathematics and presents extended treatments of mathematical topics ranging from elementary geometry through General Relativity.

CHAPTER **1**

A First Look at Logo

This chapter introduces the basic mechanics of using Logo. It describes how to evaluate simple commands and how to define and edit procedures. The examples are given in terms of using turtle graphics to draw pictures on the screen. Even though we do not, at this point, introduce more than a few commands or attempt a full explanation of the rules for writing programs, the material in this chapter and the next is sufficient to allow you to use Logo for a wide variety of interesting projects such as the ones described in Chapter 3. Try to work through this chapter at the computer keyboard, experimenting with the different features as they are introduced.

1.1. Getting Started

Figure 1.1: The Listener window as it appears when Object Logo is first started

1.2. Using Logo Commands

You start Object Logo like any other Macintosh application by double-clicking on the program icon. When Object Logo starts, it places a window on the screen called the *Listener window*. The Listener window is where you normally type Logo commands and where Logo prints its responses. Object Logo then loads the Startup file and the compiled files in the Startup Folder if they exist.

Figure 1.1 shows the Listener window as it appears when Object Logo is first started. Logo prints a welcome message followed by a line beginning with a question mark. The question mark, called a *prompt*, indicates that Logo is waiting for you to give it a command.

To give Logo a command, you type the command and press the RETURN key. For instance, to tell Logo to print the product of 37 and 67, you type the command line

PRINT 37 * 67

that is, you type the keys **P, R, I, N, T**, space, **3, 7**, space, *****, space, **6, 7**, RETURN. The computer then prints **2479**, followed by a new line with a question mark prompt, indicating readiness to accept a new command. Bear in mind that when you type a command line, it is not evaluated until you press the RETURN key. To tell Logo to print the message "Logo is a language," you type the command line

PRINT [LOGO IS A LANGUAGE]

followed by RETURN. This example illustrates how square brackets are used in Logo to group words into *lists*. You can use lists in this way to print messages on the screen, but there are many other uses for lists in Logo, and we will study these in detail in Chapters 5 and 10.

The spaces in these command lines are important, because they indicate to Logo how the line is to be broken into its component parts.[1] If you type the first command line omitting the space between the **T** and the **3** as follows:

PRINT37 * 67

then Logo will think you are telling it to evaluate a command named **PRINT37** and complain that it does not know how to do this, by responding with the error message:

You haven't told me how to PRINT37.

Figure 1.2 shows what appears in the Listener window after you give the three command lines described above, along with the computer's response to each line. The question mark shown at the beginning of each command line is the prompt typed by Logo, and the rest of the line is the command typed by the user. In this book, when we want to emphasize the difference between the characters that you type and the characters that Logo types, we print the characters that you type in boldface. For example, the first command interaction in figure 1.2 would be printed in this book as

? PRINT 37 * 67
2479

In later chapters, we will see how to write Logo programs that manipulate numbers and text. But we begin our study of Logo by investigating how to use the computer to produce drawings by issuing commands to a "object" known as a *turtle*. To set up the screen for drawing, type **CLEARSCREEN** and press RETURN. A new window, called the *Graphics window*, will appear on the screen. As shown in figure 1.3, the Graphics window will be blank, except for a small triangle in the center.

The turtle is the triangular pointer that appears at the center of the Graphics window. You make drawings by telling the turtle to move and to leave a trace of its trail. There are four basic commands for moving the turtle. The commands **FORWARD** and **BACK** make the turtle move along the direction it is pointing. Each time you give a **FORWARD** or **BACK** command, you must also specify a number that tells how far the turtle should move. The commands **RIGHT** and

Figure 1.2: Three commands typed to Object Logo and the system's responses

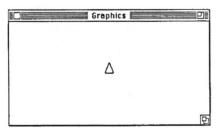

Figure 1.3: Initial appearance of the Graphics window

1.2.1. Basic Turtle Commands

---

[1] Logo has some knowledge about where it is reasonable to divide lines into component parts, even when they are not separated by spaces. For example, it knows enough to interpret the string of 5 characters **37*67** as containing three elements: the number 37, the symbol *, and the number 67. However, it is a good habit to always use spaces to separate the elements of command lines, even when this is not strictly necessary.

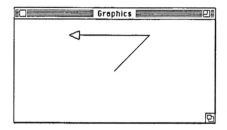

Figure 1.4: Result in the Graphics window of a simple sequence of turtle commands

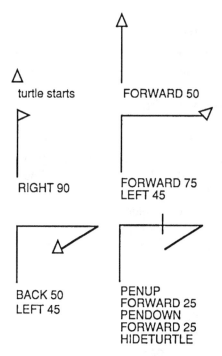

turtle starts

FORWARD 50

RIGHT 90

FORWARD 75
LEFT 45

BACK 50
LEFT 45

PENUP
FORWARD 25
PENDOWN
FORWARD 25
HIDETURTLE

Figure1.5: Drawing with the turtle

1.2.2. Error Messages

LEFT cause the turtle to rotate. **RIGHT** and **LEFT** each require you to specify the amount of rotation in degrees. Try typing the following sequence of Logo commands:

RIGHT 45
FORWARD 100
LEFT 135
FORWARD 200

This should produce the wedge-shaped drawing shown in figure 1.4. Remember to terminate each command line with RETURN and to include a space between the command word and the number. If you mistype a character, you can delete the character by pressing the DELETE key.

The number following the command is called an *input*. **FORWARD, BACK, LEFT,** and **RIGHT** each need one input. Logo commands may or may not require inputs, depending on the command. **CLEARSCREEN** is an example of a command that takes no inputs. Later we will see examples of commands that require more than one input.

If you want to move the turtle without drawing a line, give the **PENUP** command. Subsequent **FORWARD** and **BACK** commands will now make the turtle move without leaving a trail. To resume drawing, give the **PENDOWN** command. Neither **PENUP** nor **PENDOWN** takes an input. The **HIDETURTLE** command causes the turtle pointer to disappear, although the turtle is still "there" and will draw lines if the pen is down. **SHOWTURTLE** makes the pointer reappear. Figure 1.5 illustrates the use of these commands to draw a simple picture.

If you want to start over and draw a new picture, you can use the **CLEARSCREEN** command. This erases the screen and restores the turtle to its initial location at the center of the screen, pointing straight up.

If Logo cannot evaluate the input line, it replies with an error message. Logo's error messages attempt to be helpful in describing what went wrong. For example, if you try to evaluate the command line

PRINT 3 –
Logo will reply

Not enough inputs to –.

because it expects to find something after the – to be subtracted from 3. Another common error message is the result of attempting to use a command that has not been defined. For instance, if you try to evaluate

TURN 100

Logo will respond

You haven't told me how to TURN.

unless you have first defined a procedure named **TURN**.[2] The **YOU HAVEN'T TOLD ME HOW TO** error message often occurs as a result of a typing error. For example, if you type an input line like

FORWARD100

omitting the space between the **D** and the **1**, Logo responds

You haven't told me how to FORWARD100 .

because Logo reads the entire line as a single word, which it assumes is supposed to be the name of a procedure.

When Logo responds to your command with an error message, you should try to determine the reason for the error. Sometimes it is a simple typing error. If so, you can retype the line, or, if you prefer, you can edit the line: Use the up arrow key to move the cursor up to the mistyped line and press the DELETE key. This will recopy the line to the bottom of Listener window where you can edit it. Sometimes however, the reason for a Logo error may be hidden deep in the design of one of your programs. The activity of rooting out and repairing errors in programs is called *debugging*, and Logo provides debugging aids to make this task easier. These are described in section 4.3.

1.2.3. Practice with Commands

If this is your first exposure to Logo, it would be a good idea to review the material covered so far by drawing some figures using the turtle commands. Try to understand any error messages that occur. Following are some things to note in your exploring.

Abbreviations

Some of the commonly used Logo commands have abbreviations to make them easier to type. Abbreviations for some of the commands we have seen so far are

PRINT	PR
FORWARD	FD
BACK	BK
RIGHT	RT
LEFT	LT
PENUP	PU
PENDOWN	PD
HIDETURTLE	HT
SHOWTURTLE	ST

---

[2] Section 1.3 explains how to define procedures.

Multiple commands on a line

There is no restriction that each line be only a single Logo command. If you like, you can evaluate lines like

FORWARD 10 PENUP FORWARD PENDOWN

Logo will evaluate the separate commands in order, from left to right. If some command in the line causes an error, Logo will evaluate the commands up until the point of the error before typing an error message. However, single lines that contain many separate commands can be confusing, and it is generally better to use only one command per line.

The REPEAT command

One useful addition to your repertoire of Logo commands is **REPEAT. REPEAT** takes two inputs—a number and a list of commands—and repeats the commands in the list the designated number of times. For example,

REPEAT 4 [FORWARD 50 RIGHT 90]

makes the turtle draw a square. Notice that the list of commands is enclosed in square brackets. Be sure to use square brackets **[ ]**, not parentheses **( )**, for lists. This is a very simple example of how lists are used in Logo to group things. Lists are introduced in section 5.4. **REPEAT**s can be nested. For a pretty effect, try

REPEAT 10 [REPEAT 4 [FORWARD 50 RIGHT 90] RIGHT 36]

which produces the drawing shown in figure 1.6. Playing with nested **REPEAT**s can be fun, but in terms of program clarity and power, it is much better to combine commands by defining procedures, as we describe in section 1.3.

Stopping evaluation with Command-Period

When Logo is evaluating a command, typing **Command-Period** causes it to stop whatever it is doing and wait for a new command. You type **Command-Period** by holding down the key with an apple and pressing the period key. Logo types

Stopped!

and prompts for a new input line. For example, if you should start Logo evaluating some long process like

REPEAT 10000 [PRINT 1]

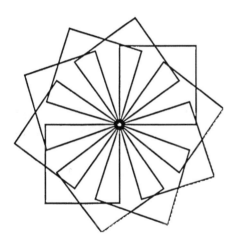

Figure 1.6: Using nested **REPEAT**s to produce a complex drawing

and then think better of it, you can halt it by pressing **Command-Period**. Another way to stop Logo is to select **Stop** from the **Logo** menu. This will have the same effect as pressing **Command-Period**.

1.3. Introduction to Procedures

You can regard Logo commands like **FORWARD, PRINT, CLEARSCREEN,** and so on, as words that the computer understands when the Logo system is started. These "built-in" words are called *primitives*. One of the most important things about the Logo language is that it makes it easy for you to teach the computer *new* words. Once you define a new word, it becomes part of the computer's working vocabulary and can be used just as if it were a primitive. You teach Logo new words by defining them in terms of words that are already known. These definitions are called *procedures*, and this section describes the simple mechanics of how to define and edit procedures. As in the previous section, the examples are drawn from turtle graphics programs.

1.3.1. Simple Procedures

The following sequence of commands makes the turtle draw a rectangular box as shown in figure 1.7.

```
FORWARD 40
RIGHT 90
FORWARD 20
RIGHT 90
FORWARD 40
RIGHT 90
FORWARD 20
```

Figure 1.7: Shape drawn by the **BOX** procedure

You can teach the computer to evaluate this sequence of commands whenever you give the command **BOX** by defining **BOX** as a procedure:

```
TO BOX
FORWARD 40
RIGHT 90
FORWARD 20
RIGHT 90
FORWARD 40
RIGHT 90
FORWARD 20
END
```

Notice first that the format of the procedure definition is

• A *title line*, which consists of the word **TO** followed by the name you choose for the procedure.

• A *body*, which is the sequence of command lines that make up the definition.

• The word **END** to indicate that this is the end of the definition.

Once **BOX** is defined, it can now be used in further definitions, such as

TO BOXES
BOX
PENUP
FORWARD 5
LEFT 90
FORWARD 15
RIGHT 90
PENDOWN
BOX
END

or

TO PINWHEEL
REPEAT 4 [BOX]
END

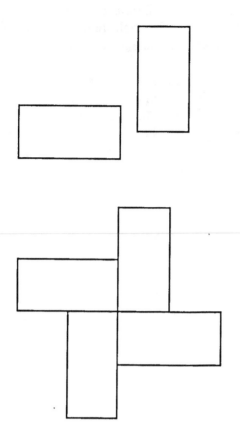

Figure 1.8: Shapes drawn by the **БOXES** and **PINWHEEL** procedures

which produce the drawings shown in figure 1.8. When a procedure is used as part of the definition of a new procedure, it is referred to as a *subprocedure* of the new procedure.

Remember that once a procedure is defined, you can consider it to be just another word that the computer "knows." You tell Logo to evaluate any of these procedures in the same way that you tell it to evaluate a primitive command—by typing the name of the command followed by RETURN.

1.3.2. Defining Procedures

The most convenient way to define procedures is to type the definitions into a separate window which you can later save as a file on a disk. To open the window select **NewFile** under the **File** menu at the top of the screen. A new *file window* will then open; the name of the window will be **Untitled**. Type the definition of **BOX** into the new window separating the lines by return. Don't forget to type **END** at the end of the definition. When you have completed the definition, go under the **Logo** menu and select **Run Selection**. At this point the message

BOX defined.

will appear in the Listener window, indicating that Logo has now "learned" your procedure definition. You must use **Run Selection** to process each procedure definition or the computer will not "learn" the definition. To try the procedure, select the Listener window and type **BOX** followed by RETURN, just like any other Logo command.

You can add new definitions to the same file window along with **BOX**. For each new procedure, choose **Run Selection**. This will run all the consecutive (non-blank) lines surrounding the current cursor location in the file window.

In general, when you define procedures, you will be moving back and forth between the Listener window and a file window. The definitions are typed in the file window. The Logo command lines that you want to run, together with Logo's responses, are typed in the Listener window. You can use the keyboard shortcuts **Command-1**, **Command-2** and **Command-3** to activate the topmost Listener, Graphics, and File window, respectively.

Changing Procedure Definitions

Suppose you want to change the definition of a procedure. For example, you may want to change the definition of **PINWHEEL** from

```
TO PINWHEEL
REPEAT 4 [BOX]
END
```

to

```
TO PINWHEEL
FORWARD 50
REPEAT 8 [RIGHT 45 BOX]
BACK 90
END
```

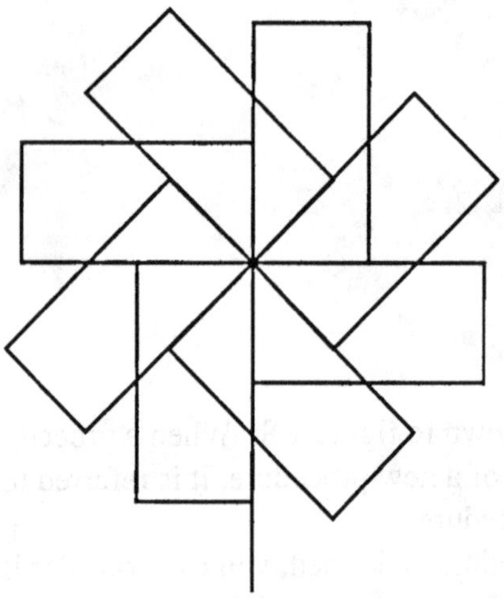

Figure 1.9: Shape drawn by the modified **PINWHEEL** procedure

so that it makes the drawing shown in figure 1.9. To do this, go back to the file window and edit the definition of **PINWHEEL**. When you have completed editing it, select the edited definition with the mouse and do **Run Selection**. Logo will reply

PINWHEEL redefined

in the Listener window.

Changing a procedure's name (by editing the title line) is equivalent to defining a new procedure with the new title. For example, if you edit the **PINWHEEL** definition to read

```
TO FAN
REPEAT 8 [RIGHT 45 BOX]
END
```

Figure 1.10: Shape drawn by the **FAN** procedure

(which draws the shape shown in figure 1.10), Logo will remember *both* **FAN** and **PINWHEEL**.

Long Lines in Procedures

Occasionally you may want to type a long procedure line, or format a single command line over more than one line so that it looks more readable. Object Logo treats any line beginning with an underscore character (_) as a continuation of the previous line. For example, you can type

```
REPEAT 10
_        [FORWARD 40 RIGHT 65
_         FORWARD 75 RIGHT 90
_         FORWARD 30]
```

instead of

```
REPEAT 10 [FORWARD 40 RIGHT 65 FORWARD 75 RIGHT 90 FORWARD 30]
```

When you reach the end of a screen line and wish to continue the command on the next line, press the tab key. The cursor will move to the next line and Logo will type an underscore and a space and you can continue typing.

1.3.3. Errors in Procedures

If Logo encounters an error while evaluating a procedure, it prints an error message. The error message gives a description of the error and the name of the procedure in which the error occurred. For example, suppose you define the procedure

```
TO BLOCK
ELL
RIGHT 90
ELL
END
```

and the definition of the subprocedure **ELL** contains a typing error (in the third line of the procedure):

```
TO ELL
FORWARD 50
RIGHT 90
FORWATD 25
END
```

Then if you give the command **BLOCK**, Logo will run until it tries to evaluate the third line in **ELL** at which point Logo will respond

You haven't told me how to FORWATD, in ELL

At this point you should edit **ELL** and correct the mistyped line.

Errors in Procedure Definitions

When Logo processes a procedure definition, it does not look for errors in the lines that make up the body of the definition. For example, if you make a typing error, as in the second line below:

```
TO PINWHEEL
REPEAT 8 [RIGXT 45 BOX]
END
```

the fact that **RIGHT** has been mistyped as **RIGXT** will cause an error when Logo attempts to *evaluate* **PINWHEEL**, not when you define the procedure.[3]

On the other hand, there are certain things that do cause errors when procedures are defined. For example, you may have mistakenly edited the procedure to remove the word **TO** from the title line or caused the definition to be badly formed in some other way. Logo will complain, for example, if you try to define a procedure with the same title as a Logo primitive. For instance, if you attempt to define a procedure named **FORWARD**, Logo will respond with

```
Can't redefine primitive FORWARD.
```

1.3.4. Defining Procedures in the Listener Window

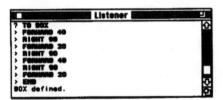

Figure 1.11: Defining a procedure in the Listener window

If you wish, you can type procedure definitions directly in the Listener window, rather than in a separate file window. When you type the title line followed by RETURN, Logo responds with a special prompt character **>**. The prompt **>** in place of the usual **?** indicates that you are defining a procedure—the lines you type are being remembered as part of the procedure definition, rather than being evaluated directly. When you type **END**, Logo responds with a message indicating that the procedure has been defined, and returns to the normal **?** prompt. Figure 1.11 shows an example of a procedure defined in this way.

Editing Procedures in Editor Windows

When you define a procedure in a file window, you can always return to that window to edit the procedure. To edit a procedure defined in the Listener window, you use the **EDIT** command. If you type, for example,

```
EDIT [BOX]
```

---

[3] One very good reason for this is that it is always possible that you *did* mean to type **RIGXT**, and you will be defining a procedure named **RIGXT** before using **PINWHEEL**. One facility that a computer language can provide to encourage sound programming practices is to make it possible to write definitions in terms of procedures that have not yet been defined.

Figure 1.12: An Editor window created by the command **EDIT [BOX]**

Logo will create a new window, called an *Editor window*, and place the text of **BOX** in it so you can edit it as shown in figure 1.12. When you close the Editor window, **BOX** will be redefined according to the edited definition.

For working through this book, we suggest that you type your procedure definitions in a file window, rather than in the Listener window or in an editor window. This way you can organize the file window so that related procedure definitions appear together, which will make your programs easier to understand. You can also use a different file window for each of your Logo projects.

1.4. Other Graphics commands

Object Logo includes a wide variety of graphics commands. This selection describes some of the ones that we have not already seen.

In addition to the turtle commands **FORWARD, BACK, LEFT,** and **RIGHT,** Logo allows you to move the turtle by specifying x, y Cartesian coordinates. The **SETPOS** command takes a list of two numbers as input and moves the turtle to the corresponding x, y screen location. There are also commands **XCOR** and **YCOR** that output the turtle's position. The **SETHEADING** command rotates the turtle so that it faces in a specified direction, and the **TOWARDS** command outputs the direction in which the turtle should be pointing in order to face a specified point. Giving the command **HOME** moves the turtle back to its initial position in the center of the screen and facing straight up. **CLEAN** erases any drawings on the screen without changing the turtle's position.

1.4.1. Drawing in Color

If you have a color monitor, you can use the **SETPENCOLOR** command to change the color of the lines that the turtle draws. You can also use the **SETBACKCOLOR** command to make the turtle draw on various background colors. The input to these commands is a number that specifies the color. Color numbers are based on the encoding scheme used by Apple QuickDraw, in which the number encodes a particular combination of red, green, and blue. The glossary and the Object Logo Reference Manual provides details on how colors are encoded. Here are the numbers that correspond to various colors:

Black	33	Blue	409
White	30	Cyan	273
Red	205	Magenta	137
Green	341	Yellow	69

For example,

SETBACKCOLOR 137
SETPENCOLOR 273

will make the background magenta, and the turtle will draw in cyan.

To save you the trouble of remembering the color numbers you can create a file with the following procedure definitions to load in whenever you want to draw in color:

```
TO BLACK
OUTPUT 33
END

TO WHITE
OUTPUT 30
END

TO RED
OUTPUT 205
END
```

and so on.[4]

With these definitions, you can now type, for example

```
SETBACKCOLOR MAGENTA
SETPENCOLOR CYAN
```

The command **SETPENSIZE** changes the size of the turtle's pen, so that it draws lines of varying height and width.

```
SETPENSIZE 4 8
```

will draw lines that are 4 pixels wide and 8 pixels high. You can also draw lines that are filled in according to a pattern, which is encoded as a list of 8 numbers. For example

```
SETPENPATTERN [238 221 187 119 238 221 187 119]
```

will draw diagonal stripes. Figures 1.13 and 1.14 show examples of different pen settings. See the glossary and the Object Logo Reference Manual for information on how to encode patterns.

1.4.2. Drawing with Patterns

Figure 1.13: Turtle figure drawn with pen size 4 8

Figure 1.14: Turtle figure drawn with pen size 4 8 and pen pattern 238 221 187 119 238 221 187 119

---

[4] This is a very simple use of the Logo **OUTPUT** command which is discussed in section 5.2.

CHAPTER **2**

Programming with Procedures

In the introduction we stressed that the ability to define procedures is one of the powerful features of the Logo language. In this chapter we explain more about how procedures can be used and, in particular, how they can be used to build up complex programs in simple steps. With the material covered in this chapter, you should have enough information about Logo to undertake many projects in turtle geometry such as the ones presented in Chapter 3.

2.1. Procedures with Inputs

The procedures discussed in section 1.3 do exactly the same thing each time they are called. Each turtle procedure draws the same drawing each time. Contrast this with a command like **FORWARD**.

FORWARD 50

does not draw exactly the same thing as

FORWARD 25

The fact that the **FORWARD** command takes an *input* is what enables you to use this one command to draw lines of all different lengths.

In Logo, you can define procedures that take inputs. Consider, for example, the following procedure, which draws a square 50 units on a side:

```
TO SQUARE
REPEAT 4 [FORWARD 50 RIGHT 90]
END
```

Whenever you give the command **SQUARE**, the turtle draws a square with side 50. You can change the definition of **SQUARE** so that it can be used to draw squares of all different sizes:

```
TO SQUARE :SIDE
REPEAT 4 [FORWARD :SIDE RIGHT 90]
END
```

The new **SQUARE** procedure takes an input that specifies the side of the square to be drawn. The procedure is evaluated just like any Logo command that takes an input, that is, to draw a square of side 50 you type

SQUARE 50

To draw a square of side 25 you type

SQUARE 25

and so on.[1]

    The definition of **SQUARE** illustrates the general rule for defining procedures that take inputs. You choose a name for the input and include it in the procedure title line, preceded by a colon.[2]

    Here's another example. You can modify the original (side 50) **SQUARE** procedure to draw a diagonal of the square, and return the turtle to its starting point. The procedure uses the fact that the length of the diagonal is the square root of 2 (about 1.4, or 7/5) times the length of the side.

TO DIAG
REPEAT 4 [FORWARD 50 RIGHT 90]
RIGHT 45
FORWARD 70
BACK 70
LEFT 45
END

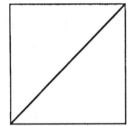

Figure 2.1: Shape drawn by the **DIAG** procedure

Figure 2.1 shows the shape drawn by this procedure. To draw the shape in all different sizes, you can use

TO DIAG :SIZE
REPEAT 4 [FORWARD :SIZE RIGHT 90]
RIGHT 45
FORWARD (:SIZE * 7) / 5
BACK (:SIZE * 7) / 5
LEFT 45
END

2.1.1. Multiple Inputs

    Logo procedures may be defined to accept more than one input. You simply choose a name for each input and include it in the title line, preceded by a colon. For example, the following two-input procedure can be used to draw rectangles of varying sizes and shapes:

---

[1]A common beginners' mistake is to type **SQUARE :50**, based on the (reasonable) misunderstanding that the colon means something like "here is your input." Instead, as we shall see below, the colon as used in **:SIDE** means "the value associated with the name **SIDE**."

[2]Logo tradition is to pronounce the colon as "dots." That is, **:SIDE** is pronounced "dots **SIDE**." Now you use the input name (with the colon) wherever you would normally use the value of the input in the procedure body.

```
TO RECTANGLE :HEIGHT :LENGTH
FORWARD :HEIGHT
RIGHT 90
FORWARD :LENGTH
RIGHT 90
FORWARD :HEIGHT
RIGHT 90
FORWARD :LENGTH
RIGHT 90
END
```

As shown in figure 2.2, executing the command

RECTANGLE 70 10

draws a long, skinny rectangle, whereas

RECTANGLE 70 70

draws a square.

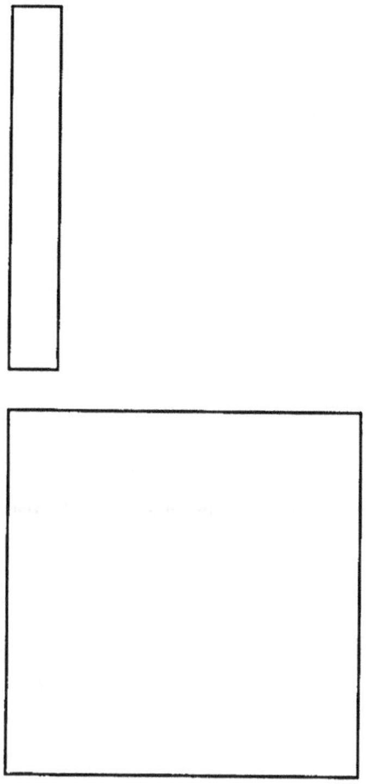

Figure 2.2: Two rectangles drawn by the **RECTANGLE** procedure

2.1.2. Inputs as Private Names

Defining a Logo procedure involves grouping together a series of commands under a *name* chosen by the programmer. Using inputs also involves naming, but in a different sense. Although a new procedure is incorporated as part of Logo's working vocabulary, the name of an input is *private* to the procedure that uses the input.

Since input names are private, different procedures may use the same names for inputs without these names interfering with each other. One way to think about this is to imagine that each time a procedure is invoked, it sets up a "private library" that associates to its input names the actual input values with which the procedure was called. When the procedure evaluates a line that contains an input name (signaled by :) it looks up the value in the library and substitutes the value for the name. For example, the previous **RECTANGLE** procedure, called with

RECTANGLE 70 10

would set up a private library as shown in figure 2.3.

The input values are associated with the input names in the order in which they appear in the title line. In this case, the first input, 70, is associated with the first input name, **HEIGHT**, and the second input, 10, with the second name, **LENGTH**.

We've already seen in Chapter 1 that the individual steps in a procedure can themselves be procedures. Since each procedure

HEIGHT	**70**
LENGTH	**10**

Figure 2.3: Private library set up by executing **RECTANGLE 70 10**

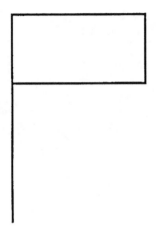

Figure 2.4: Picture drawn by
FLAG 70

maintains its own private library of input values, there is no conflict between the input names used by the different procedures. For example, here is **RECTANGLE** used as part of a procedure for drawing a flag, shown in figure 2.4:

```
TO FLAG :HEIGHT
FORWARD :HEIGHT
RECTANGLE (:HEIGHT / 2) :HEIGHT
BACK :HEIGHT
END
```

The **FLAG** procedure draws a "pole" of a specified **HEIGHT,** then draws on top of the pole a rectangle of dimensions **HEIGHT/2** by **HEIGHT,** then moves the turtle back to the base of the pole. Note the use of parentheses around **(:HEIGHT / 2).** These are not actually necessary for Logo to understand what is meant, but they make the program easier to read.[3]

Let's examine in detail what happens when you evaluate the command

FLAG 70

This creates a private library for **FLAG** in which **HEIGHT** is associated to 70, and begins evaluating the definition of **FLAG,** starting with the first line

FORWARD :HEIGHT

Looking in the private library, Logo finds that 70 is the value associated with **HEIGHT,** so it makes the turtle go **FORWARD** 70. Next it must evaluate the line

RECTANGLE (:HEIGHT / 2) :HEIGHT

To do this, Logo first determines the values of the two inputs that must be given to **RECTANGLE.** The first input is half the value of **HEIGHT,** or 35, and the second input is **HEIGHT** itself, or 70. Now **RECTANGLE** is called with inputs 35 and 70. This sets up a private library for **RECTANGLE** in which the names of **RECTANGLE**'s inputs, **HEIGHT** and **LENGTH** are associated to 35 and 70, respectively. The entire picture is as shown in Figure 2.5. Even though the name **HEIGHT** is associated with 70 in **FLAG**'s library and with 35 in **RECTANGLE**'s library there is no conflict between the two. Each procedure looks up its own values in its own library.

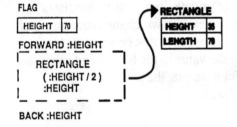

Figure 2.5: Private libraries set up by executing **FLAG 70**

---

[3] Section 5.7.2 discusses the rules for using parentheses in Logo.

The importance of private input names is that you can use a procedure without concern for the details of precisely *how it is coded,* but rather just concentrating on *what it does.* When you write the **FLAG** procedure, you can regard **RECTANGLE** as a "black box" that draws a rectangle, without worrying about what names it uses for its inputs. Indeed, as far as **FLAG** is concerned, **RECTANGLE** might have been a primitive included in the Logo system.

The technique of regarding a procedure (even a complex procedure) as a black box whose details you needn't worry about at the moment is a crucial idea in programming or, indeed, in any kind of design enterprise. Each time you define a new procedure, you can use it as a building block in more complex procedures, and in this way you can build up very complex processes in what Papert [21] refers to as "mind-size bites."

As a simple illustration, once you have defined **FLAG** you can use it to easily make a procedure that draws a flag and moves the turtle over a bit:[4]

```
TO FLAG.AND.MOVE :SIZE :DISTANCE
PENDOWN
FLAG :SIZE
PENUP
RIGHT 90
FORWARD :DISTANCE
LEFT 90
END
```

Figure 2.6: Picture drawn by ROW 30 40 4

and you can use this to draw a row of flags as in figure 2.6:

```
TO ROW :SIZE :SPACING :HOW.MANY
REPEAT :HOW.MANY [FLAG.AND.MOVE :SIZE :SPACING]
END
```

2.1.3. An ARC Procedure

As another example of using procedures with inputs, we'll consider the problem of writing a procedure to draw circular arcs. This is not only a good example of using procedures, but it is also a useful building block to have in making drawings.

The **ARC** procedure is based on making the turtle go **FORWARD** a small fixed distance, turning a small fixed angle, and repeating this over and over—this draws a good approximation to a circular arc.[5]

---

[4] The period used in a name like **FLAG.AND.MOVE** is interpreted as an ordinary character. Logo does not allow spaces to be part of procedure names, so the period is a useful way to make long names more readable.

[5] This is a fundamental idea in turtle geometry, based on the fact that a circle is a curve of constant curvature. This observation is the key to many turtle-based approaches to mathematics as described in the book by Abelson and diSessa [1].

When the turtle has turned through 360 degrees, a complete circle will have been be drawn. This leads to the following circle procedure: [6]

TO CIRCLE1
REPEAT 360 [FORWARD 1 RIGHT 1]
END

You can make this procedure more useful by giving it an input that varies the size of the circle:

TO CIRCLE2 :SIZE
REPEAT 360 [FORWARD :SIZE RIGHT 1]
END

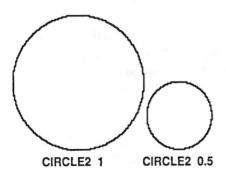

CIRCLE2 1   CIRCLE2 0.5

Figure 2.7: Circles drawn by the
CIRCLE2 procedure

Note that the turtle still turns 1 degree at each step, so varying the size of the **FORWARD** step varies the size of the circle. Figure 2.7 shows some circles drawn by the **CIRCLE2** procedure:

On the other hand, it seems even more useful to have a circle procedure whose side input specifies the radius of the circle that will be drawn. To accomplish this you can reason as follows: the **CIRCLE2** procedure draws a circle whose circumference is 360 times **SIZE**. Since the circumference of circle is equal to 2π times its radius, we have

$$360 \ \times \ \textbf{SIZE} = 2\pi \ \times \ \text{radius}$$

or

$$\textbf{SIZE} = \text{radius} \ \times \ \pi/180 = \text{radius} \ \times \ 0.0174$$

as a good approximation. Thus you can define the desired **CIRCLE** procedure using **CIRCLE2** as a subprocedure:

TO CIRCLE :RADIUS
CIRCLE2 :RADIUS * 0.0174
END

An **ARC** procedure can be implemented in the same way, except the turtle should turn only as many 1-degree steps as there are degrees in the arc. The following procedure draws circular arcs turning toward the right:

TO ARCRIGHT :RADIUS :DEGREES
ARCRIGHT1 :RADIUS * 0.0174 :DEGREES
END

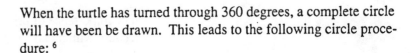

ARCRIGHT 60 90   ARCRIGHT 300 10

ARCLEFT 30 180   ARCLEFT 50 60

Figure 2.8: Circular arcs drawn by the
ARCRIGHT and **ARCLEFT** procedures

---

[6] The digit 1 included as part of the name **CIRCLE1** is interpreted as an ordinary character. It is standard practice to name minor variants of procedures by appending a number to the name.

```
TO PETAL :SIZE
ARCRIGHT :SIZE 60
RIGHT 120
ARCRIGHT :SIZE 60
RIGHT 120
END

TO FLOWER :SIZE
REPEAT 6 [PETAL :SIZE RIGHT 60]
END
```

FLOWER 50

2.1.4. Improving the Arc Procedure

```
TO RAY :SIZE
ARCLEFT :SIZE 90
ARCRIGHT :SIZE 90
ARCLEFT :SIZE 90
ARCRIGHT :SIZE 90
END


TO SUN :SIZE
REPEAT 9 [RAY :SIZE RIGHT 160]
END
```

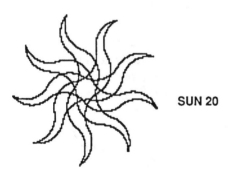

SUN 20

Figure 2.9: Simple procedures that use arcs

```
TO ARCRIGHT1 :SIZE :DEGREES
REPEAT :DEGREES  [FORWARD :SIZE RIGHT 1]
END
```

The **ARCLEFT** procedure is similar except that the turtle should turn left instead of right. Figure 2.8 shows some arcs generated by these procedures.

Once you have defined **ARCRIGHT** and **ARCLEFT,** you can use them to develop all sorts of interesting shapes. Figure 2.9 shows two examples.

The **ARCRIGHT** procedure given above draws the correct shape, but it is very slow, especially if you use it without hiding the turtle. The problem is that there are so many **FORWARD 1, LEFT 1** moves per arc. And these are mostly unnecessary, because, within the accuracy of the display screen, a regular polygon with more than, say, 20 sides is indistinguishable from a circle. For example, you can replace the **CIRCLE1** procedure by the following version, which draws a regular 36-sided polygon:

```
TO CIRCLE1
REPEAT 36 [FORWARD 10  RIGHT 10]
END
```

(Notice that you multiply the **FORWARD** step by 10 in order to keep the circle the same size as before.) Using this new **CIRCLE1,** the **CIRCLE** procedure runs about 10 times as fast and looks almost the same on the display screen.

You can do the same trick with arcs, but there is a complication. You would like to define a new **ARCRIGHT** procedure analogous to the new **CIRCLE1,** where the turtle turns in units of 10 degrees, something like:

```
TO ARCRIGHT1 :SIZE :DEGREES
REPEAT :DEGREES / 10  [FORWARD :SIZE * 10 RIGHT 10]
END
```

This works fine as long as **DEGREES** is a multiple of 10. But suppose it is not. For example, if **DEGREES** were 76, the **ARCRIGHT** procedure would draw a 70-degree arc and then stop.[7]

---

[7] In Object Logo division will produce a fraction, for instance, 76 divided by 10 yields 76/10. Asking to repeat something 76/10 times will repeat it 7 times.

You need to add an extra correction step to account for the extra 6 degrees. How far should the turtle go forward? A reasonable guess is to make it go forward 6/10 times the distance it went forward on the 10-degree turns.

In general, given an arbitrary (positive) number for **DEGREES** you make the turtle do as many

```
FORWARD :SIZE * 10
RIGHT 10
```

steps as the quotient of **DEGREES** by 10. Then you correct this by having the turtle go forward a distance proportional to the remaining number of degrees, and turn this extra angle. In implementing this, you can use the Logo **REMAINDER** primitive function, which returns the remainder of its two inputs. This yields the procedure:

```
TO ARCRIGHT1 :SIZE :DEGREES
REPEAT :DEGREES / 10 [FORWARD :SIZE * 10 RIGHT 10]
CORRECTARC :SIZE (REMAINDER :DEGREES 10)
END

TO CORRECTARC :SIZE :AMOUNT
FORWARD :SIZE * :AMOUNT
RIGHT :AMOUNT
END
```

With this new **ARCRIGHT1,** the new **ARCRIGHT** procedure, which scales the size so that the input specifies the radius of the arc, is just as before:

```
TO ARCRIGHT :RADIUS :DEGREES
ARCRIGHT1 :RADIUS * 0.0174 :DEGREES
END
```

You should make one further improvement to the arc procedure. If you use the above procedure to draw a semicircle (**DEGREES** = 180) starting with the turtle pointing straight up, the semicircle will look slightly tilted. (Try it.) This is because the turtle goes forward (straight up) before doing any turning, so the first small line is vertical. Similarly, the turtle does its final 10-degree turn after drawing the last line, so the last line of the semicircle is not vertical. This asymmetry accounts for the lopsidedness. One way to fix this is to have the turtle turn 5 degrees before doing any turning and then turn back 5 degrees after the arc is done. The resulting arc is then more symmetrically oriented with respect to the turtle's initial and final headings:

```
TO ARCRIGHT :RADIUS :DEGREES
RIGHT 5
ARCRIGHT1 :RADIUS * 0.0174 :DEGREES
LEFT 5
END
```

2.2. Repetition and Recursion

We've already seen the use of the Logo **REPEAT** command to repeat some series of steps some fixed number of times. Another way to make something repeat is to define a procedure that includes a call to itself as the final line. For example,

```
TO SQUARE :SIZE
FORWARD :SIZE
RIGHT 90
SQUARE :SIZE
END
```

makes the turtle move in a square pattern over and over again until you stop it by hand.[8]

You can think of the way this procedure works as a kind of joke—the steps of a procedure can include calls to any procedure, so why not call the procedure itself? In this case, the definition of **SQUARE** is "go forward, turn right, and then do **SQUARE** again." And this last step entails going forward, turning right, and then doing **SQUARE** again, and so on forever.[9]

One disadvantage of this **SQUARE** as opposed to the one we have been previously using,

```
TO SQUARE :SIZE
REPEAT 4 [FORWARD :SIZE RIGHT 90]
END
```

is that it goes on indefinitely and so is not a good building block to use in making more complex drawings. On the other hand, this kind of indefinite repetition can be useful in situations in which you do not know (or cannot easily figure out) how many times to repeat some sequence of steps. The following program is an excellent example:

```
TO POLY :SIDE :ANGLE
FORWARD :SIDE
RIGHT :ANGLE
POLY :SIDE :ANGLE
END
```

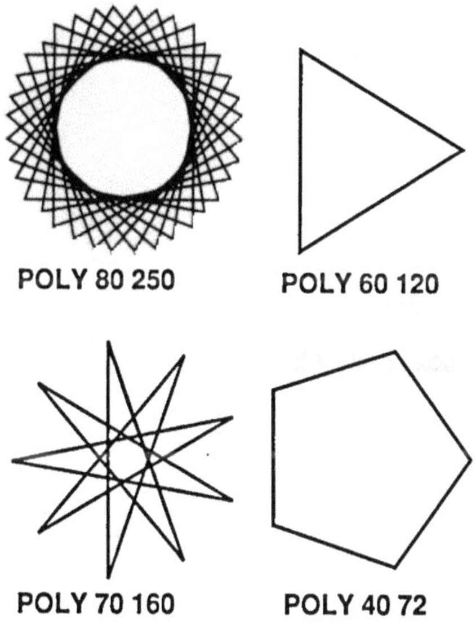

POLY 80 250   POLY 60 120

POLY 70 160   POLY 40 72

Figure 2.10: Shapes drawn by the **POLY** program

Figure 2.10 shows some of the many figures drawn by **POLY** as the angle varies. They are all closed figures, but the number sides that must be drawn before the figure closes depends in a complicated

---

[8] Remember that you can stop a logo procedure by hand by pressing **Command-Period** or by selecting **Stop** from the **Logo** menu at the top of the screen.

[9] Compare: If a genie appears and offers you three wishes, you should use your third wish to wish for three more wishes.

way upon the **ANGLE** input to the program.[10] Using the indefinite repeat you can draw them all with a single simple procedure.

Recursion is the programming word for the ability to use the term **POLY** as part of the definition of **POLY,** or in general, to write procedures that call themselves. [11]

2.2.1. Thinking about Recursion

The recursive procedures above have a very simple form—they merely repeat an unchangeable cycle over and over again. Recursion is a much more powerful idea and can be used to obtain much more complicated effects. We shall meet many examples. To take just a small step beyond the purely repetitive kind of recursion, consider

```
TO COUNTDOWN :NUMBER
PRINT :NUMBER
COUNTDOWN :NUMBER – 1
END
```

Let's examine what happens if you give the command

```
COUNTDOWN 10
```

To understand the effect of this command, look back at the definition of the **COUNTDOWN** procedure. You see that it needs an input and that it uses the name **NUMBER** for this input. In this case, you have given 10 as the input, so the procedure takes **NUMBER** to be 10.[12]

The first line says

PRINT :NUMBER

so it prints **10** and goes on to the next line, which is

COUNTDOWN :NUMBER – 1

or, in this case

COUNTDOWN 9

---

[10] This phenomenon forms the basis for a number of mathematical investigations involving symmetry and number theory, described in Abelson and diSessa [1].

[11] Languages like Fortran and (most versions of) BASIC do not allow recursion because the implementation of a computer language is simplified if one can assume that there are no recursive functions.

[12] Using the terminology introduced in section 2.1.2 we would say that **COUNT-DOWN** sets up a private library in which the name **NUMBER** is associated with 10.

This order causes the same effect as if you had typed in the command

COUNTDOWN 9

which would be to print 9 and then give the order

COUNTDOWN 8

and so on ... In sum, the effect of

COUNTDOWN 10

is to print 10, 9, 8, 7, 6, 5, 4, 3, 2, 1,0, –1, –2, ... until you stop the process by typing **Command-Period.**

Another example of the same programming technique is the following modification of the **POLY** program.

```
TO POLYSPI :SIDE :ANGLE
FORWARD :SIDE
RIGHT :ANGLE
POLYSPI (:SIDE + 3) :ANGLE
END
```

Giving the command

POLYSPI 0 90

leads to the sequence of turtle moves

```
FORWARD 0
RIGHT 90
FORWARD 3
RIGHT 90
FORWARD 6
RIGHT 90
FORWARD 9
RIGHT 90
```

POLYSPI 5 120

POLYSPI 5 144

Figure 2.11: Shapes drawn by the **POLYSPI** program

which produces a square-like spiral.[13] By changing the **ANGLE** input you can draw all sorts of spiral shapes, as shown in figure 2.11. Part of the power of recursion is the fact that such simple programs can lead to such varied, unexpected results.

---

[13] Or "squiral," as it was dubbed by a 5th grade Logo programmer who discovered this figure.

2.2.2. Conditional Commands and STOP

Suppose you want **COUNTDOWN** to stop before printing 0. You can do this as follows:

```
TO COUNTDOWN :NUMBER
IF :NUMBER = 0 [STOP]
PRINT :NUMBER
COUNTDOWN :NUMBER – 1
END
```

The **IF** statement is used in Logo to perform tests, in this case to test whether the value of **NUMBER** is zero. If so, the **COUNTDOWN** procedure **STOP**s. This is, rather than continuing with the next line in the procedure, it returns control to wherever the procedure was originally called from. So in response to the command

COUNTDOWN 5

the computer prints 5, 4, 3, 2, 1 and prompts for a new command.

Keep in mind that the idea of **STOP** is that when a procedure stops, the next command that gets executed is the one after the command that called the procedure. For example,

```
TO BLASTOFF
COUNTDOWN 10
FORWARD 100
END
```

counts down from 10 to 1 and then moves the turtle.[14]

The **IF** statement is called a *conditional expression*. It has the form

IF {some condition is true} {do some action}

The action to be performed is enclosed in brackets, similar to **REPEAT**.

The kinds of conditions that can be tested are generated by Logo operations called *predicates*. Predicates are things whose value is either true or false. **COUNTDOWN** uses =, which is true if the two things it is comparing are equal. Two other predicates are >, which tests whether the number on its left is greater than the number on its right, and <, which tests for less than. These three predicates deal with numbers.[15] Logo includes other predicates for dealing with other kinds of data. It is also easy to define your own special-purpose predicates (see section 5.6).

---

[14] This stopping behavior is just what normally happens after a procedure executes its final line. If you like, you can imagine that every procedure includes a **STOP** command at its end.

[15] Actually, = can be used for testing equality of any two pieces of Logo data.

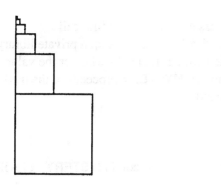

Figure 2.12: Picture drawn by **TOWER 60**

Here is a turtle program based on the **COUNTDOWN** model.

```
TO TOWER :SIZE
IF :SIZE < 1 [STOP]
SQUARE :SIZE
FORWARD :SIZE TOWER :SIZE / 2
END
```

It draws a tower of squares that get smaller and smaller and stops when the squares get very tiny, as shown in figure 2.12.

2.2.3. Thinking Harder about Recursion

The recursion examples we have seen so far, in which the recursive call is the final step in the procedure, can be readily viewed as a kind of generalized repetition.[16]   Other uses of recursion can be much more powerful but, unfortunately, much harder to understand. Let's compare the **COUNTDOWN** procedure from Section 2.2.2:

```
TO COUNTDOWN :NUMBER
IF :NUMBER = 0 [STOP]
PRINT :NUMBER
COUNTDOWN :NUMBER – 1
END
```

with the following similar-looking procedure:

```
TO MYSTERY :NUMBER
IF :NUMBER = 0 [STOP]
MYSTERY :NUMBER – 1
PRINT :NUMBER
END
```

As we saw,

COUNTDOWN 3

prints 3, 2, 1. In contrast

MYSTERY 3

prints 1, 2, 3. Most people find this very hard to understand.

---

[16] The special case of recursion in which the recursive call is the final step is sometimes called *tail recursion*. Logo includes techniques for implementing tail recursion efficiently, so that a tail recursive procedure can effectively run "forever" without running out of storage.

Let's trace through the process carefully. You first call **MYSTERY** with the input 3, and **MYSTERY** sets up a private library in which **NUMBER** is associated with 3. It checks whether the value of **NUMBER** is 0, which it is not, so **MYSTERY** proceeds to the next line which produces the command

MYSTERY 2

Now let's stop and think. Eventually this second **MYSTERY** call will stop, and the original

MYSTERY 3

procedure will have to continue with the next command after the call. But this means that there will have to be, in some sense, *two* **MYSTERY** procedures existing at once—the one called by the command

MYSTERY 2

and the original one called by the command

MYSTERY 3

which is waiting for the other **MYSTERY** to stop, so it can continue. Moreover, each **MYSTERY** has its *own* value for **NUMBER**— **NUMBER** is 2 for one and 3 for the other. Each **MYSTERY** must maintain a *separate* private library.[17] The situation is shown in figure 2.13.

Let's go on. The first thing that the

MYSTERY 2

procedure does is check whether the value for **NUMBER** is equal to 0. Since this is not the case, **MYSTERY** gives the command

MYSTERY 1

and so now there are *three* **MYSTERY** procedures! And

MYSTERY 1

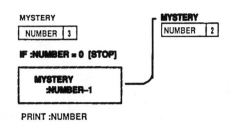

MYSTERY
| NUMBER | 3 |

IF :NUMBER = 0 [STOP]

MYSTERY
:NUMBER–1

PRINT :NUMBER

MYSTERY
| NUMBER | 2 |

Figure 2.13: Beginning evaluation of **MYSTERY 3**

---

[17] In other words, the private library is associated, not with a procedure, but with a given call to a procedure (or what is technically called an *activation* to call a procedure).

does a test and calls up yet another

MYSTERY 0

which makes four **MYSTERY** calls all existing at once as shown in figure 2.14. Note that so far nothing has been printed. All that has happened is that **MYSTERY** procedures have called up more **MYSTERY** procedures.

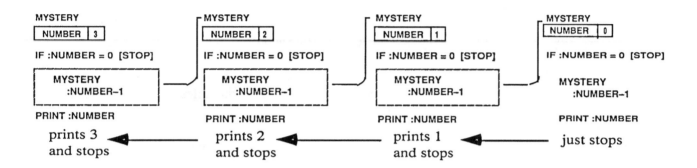

Figure 2.14: Complete evaluation of **MYSTERY 3**

Now

MYSTERY 0

performs its test and finds that the value of **NUMBER** is indeed 0. So it **STOP**s and the process continues with the procedure that called it, namely,

MYSTERY 1

This **MYSTERY** now proceeds with the next line after the call, which says to print the value of **NUMBER**. Since **NUMBER** is 1 (in *this* **MYSTERY**'s private library) it prints 1. Now it is done and so returns to the procedure that called it, namely

MYSTERY 2

This **MYSTERY** now continues with the line after the call, which says to print **NUMBER**. Since **NUMBER** is 2 (in *this* private library) it prints 2 and returns to its caller, namely,

MYSTERY 3

which prints 3 and returns to its caller, which is the main Logo command level.

Whew! Try going through this example again step by step, referring to figure 2.14. In essence, this complex process is doing nothing more than unwinding the following rule:

• When a procedure is called, the calling procedure waits until the second procedure stops, and then continues with the next instruction after the call.

Recursion, however, forces us to appreciate all the ramifications of this simple sounding rule. In particular,

• There may be several instances (or "activations") of the "same" procedure all coexisting at once.

• Each procedure activation has a *separate* private library, so the "same" name maybe associated with different values in different procedure activations.

• The order in which things happen can be very confusing.[18]

2.2.4. Drawing Trees

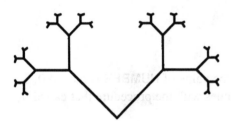

Figure 2.15: A binary tree

As another example of complex use of recursion, let's look at a program that draws a *binary tree*, as in figure 2.15.

Think about how you would describe this figure. One way to do it would be to say something like "the tree is a vee-shape with a smaller tree at each tip. And each smaller tree is a vee-shape with a still smaller tree at each of its tips, and so on." This is a *recursive description* of the tree. You can translate this description into a *recursive procedure* that draws the figure. You start with the following commands that make the turtle draw a vee-shape of a certain length and return to its initial position and heading:

```
LEFT 45
FORWARD :LENGTH
BACK :LENGTH
RIGHT 90
FORWARD :LENGTH
BACK :LENGTH
LEFT 45
```

This is the basic vee-shape of the tree. Now, according to the recursive description, the entire tree consists of this vee with smaller vees (say, half as big) drawn at each tip. So the **TREE** procedure should be something like

---

[18] More specifically, things happen in the reverse order from the way one might expect. This is a consequence of the fact that the last procedure called is the first one to stop.

```
TO TREE :LENGTH
LEFT 45
FORWARD :LENGTH
TREE :LENGTH / 2
BACK :LENGTH
RIGHT 90
FORWARD :LENGTH
TREE :LENGTH / 2
BACK :LENGTH
LEFT 45
END
```

But this doesn't quite work. Consider—if you call **TREE** with an input of 20, this will make the turtle go **LEFT 45, FORWARD 20** and call

TREE 10

which will make the turtle go **LEFT 45, FORWARD 10** and call

TREE 5

and so on forever.[19] This is something like the forever-running **COUNTDOWN** procedure of section 2.2.2, or even more like the chain of **MYSTERY** procedures in section 2.2.3, in that no procedure finishes until the last one to be called has stopped. What you need is a *stop rule* to keep the process from going on forever. You can make the process stop by having the procedure just stop without drawing anything if **LENGTH** is very small:

```
TO TREE :LENGTH
IF :LENGTH < 2 [STOP]
LEFT 45
FORWARD :LENGTH
TREE :LENGTH / 2
BACK :LENGTH
RIGHT 90
FORWARD :LENGTH
TREE :LENGTH / 2
BACK :LENGTH
LEFT 45
END
```

You can modify the **TREE** procedure to produce a procedure **TREE1**, in which the subtree branches have the same length as the original branches, rather than half the length. If you do this,

---

[19] That is, until Logo runs out of storage.

however, then the branches of successive subtrees will not get smaller and smaller, which means that you cannot use the same stop rule as in **TREE**. A different strategy for providing a stop rule is to include for **TREE1** an extra input, **DEPTH**, which determines the "depth" to which the tree is drawn. Each tree of a given depth spawns two subtrees of depth one less. When the **TREE** procedure is called with **DEPTH** equal to 0, it just stops without drawing:

```
TO TREE1 :LENGTH :DEPTH
IF :DEPTH = 0 [STOP]
LEFT 45
FORWARD :LENGTH
TREE1 :LENGTH :DEPTH–1
BACK :LENGTH
RIGHT 90
FORWARD :LENGTH
TREE1 :LENGTH :DEPTH–1
BACK :LENGTH
LEFT 45
END
```

Thinking in terms of recursive descriptions can take a lot of getting used to, and the programs can be subtle. One especially subtle point about the **TREE** program is the final **BACK** and **LEFT** moves, which are needed to restore the turtle to its initial heading so that the different calls to **TREE** will fit together correctly. On the other hand, many seemingly complex designs have simple recursive descriptions and can be drawn by remarkably brief programs. The design of recursive turtle programs for drawing complex patterns is discussed extensively in Abelson and diSessa [1].

To illustrate the flavor of recursive designs, here is a modification to **TREE1**, in which the left branch of each vee is twice as long as the right branch. We'll also allow the angle of the vee to be varied as an input. Figure 2.16 shows some of the patterns that result.

```
TO NEW.TREE :LENGTH :ANGLE :DEPTH
IF :DEPTH = 0 [STOP]
LEFT :ANGLE
FORWARD 2 * :LENGTH
NEW.TREE :LENGTH :ANGLE :DEPTH – 1
BACK 2 * :LENGTH
RIGHT 2 * :ANGLE
FORWARD :LENGTH
NEW.TREE :LENGTH :ANGLE :DEPTH – 1
BACK :LENGTH
LEFT :ANGLE
END
```

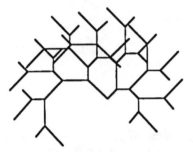

NEW.TREE 10 45 5

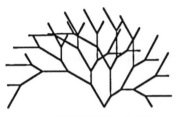

NEW.TREE 10 30 5

NEW.TREE 10 15 6

Figure 2.16: Some figures drawn by the **NEW.TREE** procedure

CHAPTER **3**

Projects in Turtle Geometry

Here are some projects that use Turtle Geometry. Refer to other portions of this text for help in defining or editing programs. Feel free to change programs that are offered and to design new programs.

Here is a square procedure.

```
TO SQUARE
REPEAT 4 [ FORWARD 60  RIGHT 90 ]
END
```

Here are two square procedures designed to allow variable size. The triangles show the turtle's initial position.

```
TO LSQUARE :SIZE
FORWARD :SIZE
LEFT 90
FORWARD :SIZE
LEFT 90
FORWARD :SIZE
LEFT 90
FORWARD :SIZE
LEFT 90
END
```

or

```
TO LSQUARE :SIZE
REPEAT 4 [ FORWARD :SIZE LEFT 90 ]
END
```

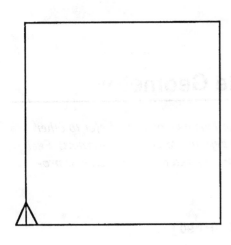

```
TO RSQUARE :SIZE
FORWARD :SIZE
RIGHT 90
FORWARD :SIZE
RIGHT 90
FORWARD :SIZE
RIGHT 90
FORWARD :SIZE
RIGHT 90
END
```

or

```
TO RSQUARE :SIZE
REPEAT 4 [ FORWARD :SIZE RIGHT 90 ]
END
```

Some procedures using RSQUARE and recursion.

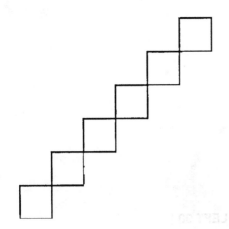

```
TO MOVE :SIZE
FORWARD :SIZE
RIGHT 90
FORWARD :SIZE
LEFT 90
END
```

```
TO STAIRS :SIZE
RSQUARE :SIZE
MOVE :SIZE
STAIRS :SIZE
END
```

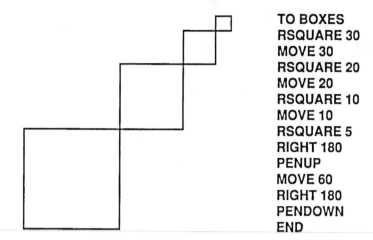

```
TO BOXES
RSQUARE 30
MOVE 30
RSQUARE 20
MOVE 20
RSQUARE 10
MOVE 10
RSQUARE 5
RIGHT 180
PENUP
MOVE 60
RIGHT 180
PENDOWN
END
```

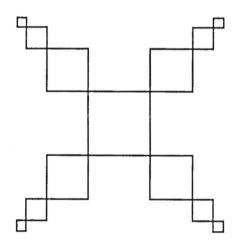

```
TO MANYBOXES
BOXES
FORWARD 30
RIGHT 90
MANYBOXES
END
```

Some ideas for using square procedures.

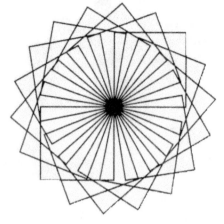

```
TO SPINSQUARES :SIZE
RSQUARE :SIZE
RIGHT 20
SPINSQUARES :SIZE
END
```

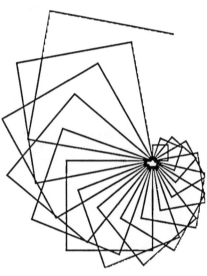

```
TO GROWSQUARES :SIZE
RSQUARE :SIZE
RIGHT 20
GROWSQUARES :SIZE + 5
END
```

A rectangle procedure designed to allow variable size and some examples that use it.

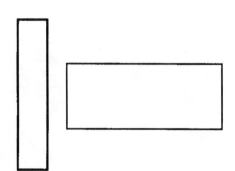

```
TO RECTANGLE :LENGTH :WIDTH
FORWARD :LENGTH
RIGHT 90
FORWARD :WIDTH
RIGHT 90
FORWARD :LENGTH
RIGHT 90
FORWARD :WIDTH
RIGHT 90
END
```

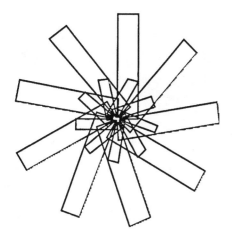

```
TO FLOWER
RECTANGLE 50 10
RIGHT 20
RECTANGLE 5 20
RIGHT 20
FLOWER
END
```

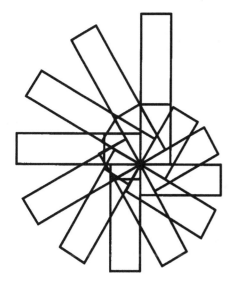

```
TO SPINRECS :SIZE
IF :SIZE < 10 [STOP]
RECTANGLE :SIZE 20
LEFT 30
SPINRECS :SIZE – 5
END
```

Examples using RSQUARE and
RECTANGLE.

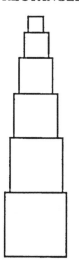

```
TO HOP :SIZE
FORWARD :SIZE
RIGHT 90
FORWARD 3
LEFT 90
END
```

```
TO TELESCOPE :SIZE
IF :SIZE < 6 [STOP]
RSQUARE :SIZE
HOP :SIZE
```

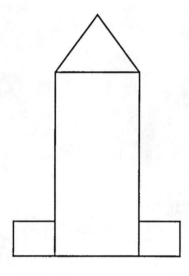

```
TELESCOPE :SIZE – 6
END
TO ROCKTOP
LEFT 30
FORWARD 30
LEFT 120
FORWARD 30
END

TO ROCKET
RECTANGLE 80 30
LEFT 90
RECTANGLE 15 15
BACK 30
RIGHT 90
RECTANGLE 15 15
FORWARD 80
ROCKTOP
END
```

Here are some examples that use a triangle procedure.

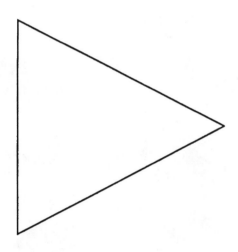

```
TO TRI
REPEAT 3 [FORWARD 70 RIGHT 120]
END
```

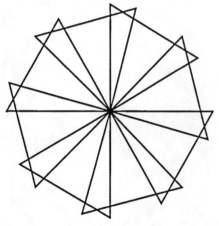

```
TO TRISTUFF
REPEAT 8 [TRI RIGHT 45]
END
```

A triangle procedure designed to
allow variable size and an example
that uses it.

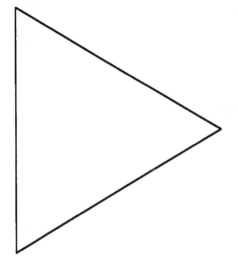

```
TO TRIANGLE :SIZE
FORWARD :SIZE
RIGHT 120
FORWARD :SIZE
RIGHT 120
FORWARD :SIZE
RIGHT 120
END
```

This procedure is different in design
but has a similar result.

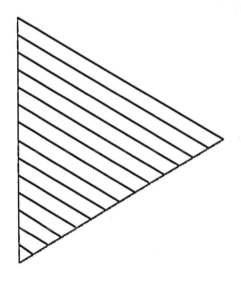

```
TO FLUFF :SIZE
IF :SIZE < 10 [STOP]
TRIANGLE :SIZE
FLUFF :SIZE – 10
END
```

Some more triangle examples.

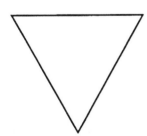

```
TO NEWTRIANGLE :SIZE
LEFT 30
TRIANGLE :SIZE
RIGHT 30
END
```

```
TO CREEP :SIZE
PENUP
FORWARD :SIZE
PENDOWN
END
```

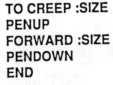

```
TO LOOPS :SIZE
NEWTRIANGLE :SIZE
CREEP :SIZE
RIGHT 60
LOOPS :SIZE
END
```

```
TO NEWLOOP :SIZE
IF :SIZE < 20 [STOP]
NEWTRIANGLE :SIZE
CREEP :SIZE/2
RIGHT 60
NEWLOOP :SIZE – 5
END
```

And one more example.

```
TO LEFTANT
LEFT 15
FORWARD 30
LEFT 120
FORWARD 15
BACK 15
RIGHT 120
BACK 30
RIGHT 15
END
```

```
TO RIGHTANT
RIGHT 15
FORWARD 30
RIGHT 120
FORWARD 15
BACK 15
LEFT 120
BACK 30
LEFT 15
END
```

```
TO ANTS
RIGHTANT
LEFTANT
END
```

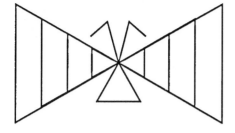

```
TO WING
TRIANGLE 80
TRIANGLE 60
TRIANGLE 40
TRIANGLE 20
END

TO BUTTERFLY
RIGHT 60
WING
RIGHT 180
WING
RIGHT 120
ANTS
RIGHT 150
TRIANGLE 30
END
```

RCP and LCP are abbreviations for "Right Circle Piece" and "Left Circle Piece." RARC and LARC stand for "right arc" and "left arc." A circle can be made from pieces of either left or right arcs, leaving the turtle at the left-most or right-most point of the circle.

```
TO RCP :R
RIGHT 5
FORWARD :R * (3.14159 / 18 )
RIGHT 5
END
```

```
TO LCP :R
LEFT 5
FORWARD :R * (3.14159 / 18 )
LEFT 5
END
```

```
TO RARC :R
REPEAT 9 [RCP :R]
END
```

```
TO LARC :R
REPEAT 9 [LCP :R]
END
```

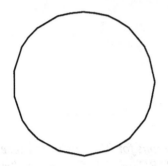

```
TO RCIRCLE :R
REPEAT 36 [RCP :R]
END

TO LCIRCLE :R
REPEAT 36 [LCP :R]
END
```

Examples using circle procedures.

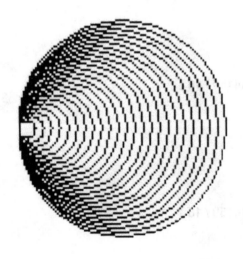

```
TO SHRINKCIRCLE :SIZE
IF :SIZE < 4 [STOP]
RCIRCLE :SIZE
SHRINKCIRCLE :SIZE – 2
END
```

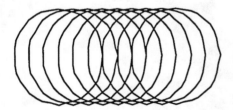

```
TO RSLINKY :SIZE
RCIRCLE :SIZE
PENUP RIGHT 90 FORWARD 10 LEFT 90 PENDOWN
RSLINKY :SIZE
END
```

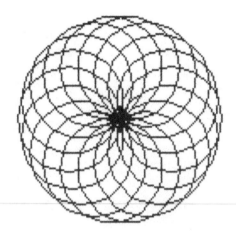

```
TO SPINSLINK :SIZE
RCIRCLE :SIZE
RIGHT 20
SPINSLINK :SIZE
END
```

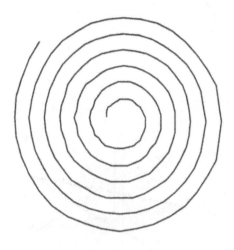

```
TO GROWCIRCLE :SIZE
REPEAT 4 [RCP :SIZE]
GROWCIRCLE :SIZE + 1
END
```

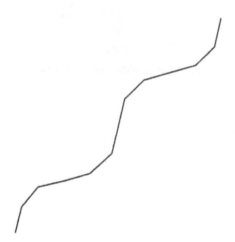

```
TO RAY :SIZE
RARC :SIZE
LARC :SIZE
RARC :SIZE
LARC :SIZE
END
```

```
TO SUN :SIZE
RAY :SIZE
RIGHT 160
SUN :SIZE
END
```

POLY procedures have variable size and angle. Here are some examples.

```
TO POLY :SIDE :ANGLE
FORWARD :SIDE
RIGHT :ANGLE
POLY :SIDE :ANGLE
END
```

POLY

SIDE = 100 ANGLE = 156

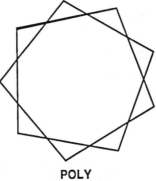

POLY

SIDE = 70 ANGLE = 80

POLY

SIDE = 100 ANGLE = 160

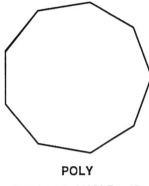

POLY
SIDE = 40 ANGLE = 40

POLY
SIDE = 100 ANGLE = 144

POLYSTEP is a piece of a POLY procedure. Here are some examples using it.

```
TO POLYSTEP :SIDE :ANGLE
FORWARD :SIDE
RIGHT :ANGLE
END
```

```
TO TWOPOLY :SIDE1 :ANGLE1 :SIDE2 :ANGLE2
POLYSTEP :SIDE1 :ANGLE1
POLYSTEP :SIDE2 :ANGLE2
TWOPOLY :SIDE1 :ANGLE1 :SIDE2 :ANGLE2
END
```

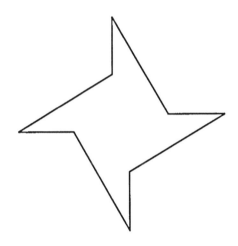

SIDE1 = 30   ANGLE1 = 60   SIDE2 = 60   ANGLE2 = 210

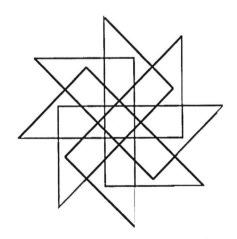

SIDE1 = 30   ANGLE1 = 90   SIDE2 = 50   ANGLE2 = 135

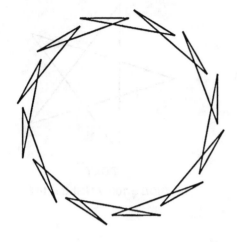

SIDE1 = 25   ANGLE1 = 190   SIDE2 = 50   ANGLE2 = 200

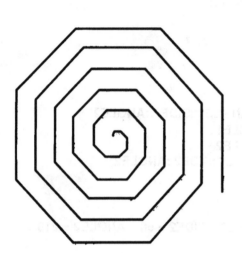

```
TO POLYSTEP :SIDE :ANGLE
FORWARD :SIDE
RIGHT :ANGLE
END

TO POLYSPIRAL :SIDE :ANGLE :INC
POLYSTEP :SIDE :ANGLE
POLYSPIRAL (:SIDE + :INC) :ANGLE :INC
END
```

SIDE = 1   ANGLE = 45   INCREMENT = 1

More programs using POLYSTEP.
You may need to change the
incrementing value inside of the
procedure, that is, the value being
added to the side each time the
program recurses.

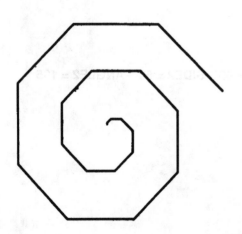

SIDE = 1   ANGLE = 45   INCREMENT = 3

SIDE = 5   ANGLE = 120   INCREMENT = 3

Here's an example that begins by defining a shape and uses it to make a more interesting shape.

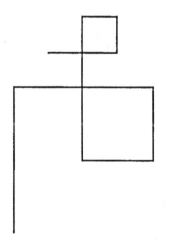

```
TO DESIGN
FORWARD 40
RIGHT 90
FORWARD 40
RIGHT 90
FORWARD 20
RIGHT 90
FORWARD 20
RIGHT 90
FORWARD 40
RIGHT 90
FORWARD 10
RIGHT 90
FORWARD 10
RIGHT 90
FORWARD 20
END
```

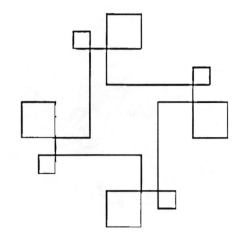

```
TO DESIGN4
DESIGN
DESIGN
DESIGN
DESIGN
END
```

```
TO CRYSTAL
DESIGN
LEFT 45
FORWARD 35
CRYSTAL
END
```

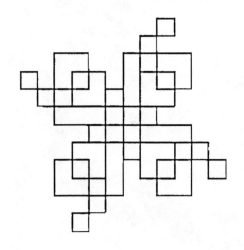

```
TO JENGU
DESIGN
DESIGN
LEFT 90
JENGU
END
```

Here are some programs using
INSPI. Try various inputs.

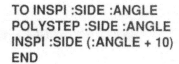

```
TO INSPI :SIDE :ANGLE
POLYSTEP :SIDE :ANGLE
INSPI :SIDE (:ANGLE + 10)
END
```

SIDE = 15   ANGLE = 1

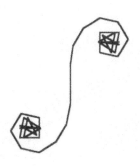

SIDE = 15   ANGLE = 10

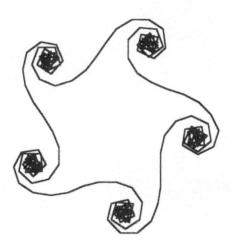

SIDE = 10   ANGLE = 3

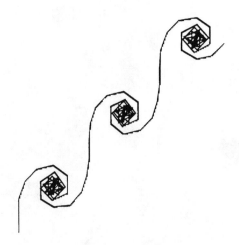

SIDE = 10   ANGLE = 5

Here is a sequence of procedures that start with a leaf (VEE) and end with a forest (TREES).

TO VEE
LEFT 45
FORWARD 20
BACK 20
RIGHT 90
FORWARD 20
BACK 20
LEFT 45
END

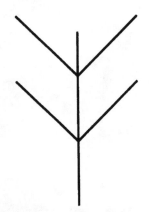

TO BRANCH
FORWARD 15
VEE
FORWARD 15
VEE
FORWARD 10
BACK 40
END

TO BUSH
LEFT 60
REPEAT 6 [BRANCH RIGHT 20]
BRANCH
LEFT 60
END

```
TO GREENTREE
FORWARD 50
BUSH
BACK 50
END
```

```
TO MOVE
PENUP
RIGHT 90
FORWARD 80
LEFT 90
PENDOWN
END
```

```
TO TREES
REPEAT 3 [GREENTREE MOVE]
END
```

Here are some project ideas using the procedures you have already seen. Feel free to make up your own projects.

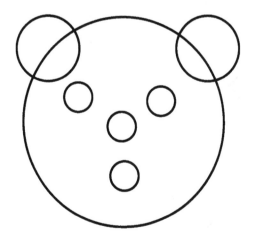

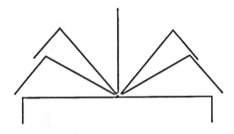

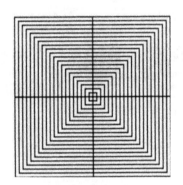

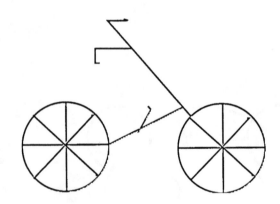

CHAPTER **4**

Workspace, Filing, and Debugging

When you use Logo, you can think of the computer as having two memories. The first memory, called *workspace*, is where Logo keeps track of the procedures and variables you have defined. Each time you define a procedure or assign a value to a name, that information becomes part of the workspace. When you quit Logo, the information in the workspace is destroyed. The second, and more permanent memory consists of files that you save on disk.

One way to use files with Logo is to type your procedure definitions into a file window as explained in section 1.3.2. When you are finished for the day, you can save the contents of the file window as a file on disk. The next time you use Logo, you can load your saved procedures and continue where you left off. You can maintain a number of different files for different projects you are working on.

Another way to use the file system is to define your procedures in the Listener window, and edit them in an Edit window as described in section 1.3.4. This way, you will not see a complete listing of all of your procedures (as you would in a file window), but the procedures will still be part of your workspace. When you are finished for the day, you can save your entire workspace in a disk file that you can load the next time you use Logo.

4.1. Managing Workspace

The Logo system includes commands for examining and deleting various parts of the workspace. These are useful for keeping track of which procedures are currently defined and for getting rid of unwanted definitions.

4.1.1. PRINTOUT

The basic command for examining workspace is **PRINTOUT** (abbreviated **PO**). If you type **PO** followed by the name of a procedure, Logo prints the definition of the procedure. **PO** can also take a list of procedure names as input, in which case it prints the definitions of all procedures in the list. For example,

PO "SQUARE

makes Logo print the definition of **SQUARE**, and

PO [SQUARE TRIANGLE]

makes Logo print the definitions of **SQUARE** and **TRIANGLE**.

PO also has a few variants:

POTS prints the titles of all procedures in workspace.

PONS prints the names and associated values in the global library.

POPS prints the definitions of all procedures in workspace.

POALL prints both names and procedures.

4.1.2. ERASE

The **ERASE** command (abbreviated **ER**) gets rid of parts of workspace. **ERASE** followed by a procedure name removes the definition of the procedure. As with **PO**, **ERASE** can also take as input a list of procedures to be erased. If you are typing your procedure definitions into a file window, then if you erase a definition from workspace, you should also cut it from the file window. Otherwise it will be defined again the next time the file is loaded.

The following variants of **ERASE** are similar to those for **PO**:

ERNS erases the names and associated values from the global library.

ERPS erases the definitions of all procedures from workspace.

ERALL erases all names and procedures.

4.1.3. Burying Procedures and Names

Sometimes it is useful to have parts of the workspace "hidden," so they are not visible to printout and erase commands. For example, you might wish to provide a set of Logo procedures for use as programming aids by beginning users, and you would like these procedures to appear as built-in primitives as far as the beginning users are concerned.

A procedure that is hidden like this is said to be "buried." A buried procedure can be used just like any other procedure, but it will not be listed by **POTS** or **POPS**, and it will not be erased by **ERPS** and **ERALL**. Similarly, a buried name will not be listed by **PONS**, erased by **ERNS**. Buried procedures and names will also not be saved as part of the workspace when you use the **SAVE** command (see section 4.2.1). To bury an item, use the **BURY** command. Once an item has been buried, you can "unbury" it with **UNBURY**.

4.2. Files

As explained at the beginning of this chapter, there are two different ways you can use files for saving your work. In *file-based programming,* you type definitions into file windows and save these files explicitly. In *workspace-based programming*, you define procedures in the Listener window, and then save workspace all at once. Workspace-based programming is easier for beginning users, because you don't have to think about file windows. File-based programming is more convenient for most applications, however, because you can control the arrangement of procedures within a file, or use multiple files to split up large programs into manageable pieces.

4.2.1. Commands for Workspace-based Programming

The **SAVE** command will save all procedures and names in workspace into a designated file. For example,

SAVE "HardDisk:Stuff

will save the workspace contents in a file named **Stuff** on the hard disk. Unless you are using **SAVE** as part of a procedure, it is simpler to save the workspace by choosing **Save Workspace As...** from the Logo menu. This will display a dialog box that prompts you for the file name, and will save the workspace in that file.

The **LOAD** command takes a file name as input and loads the contents of the file into workspace. Again, unless you are using **LOAD** inside a procedure, it is simpler to choose **Load...** from the Logo menu, and select the name of the file to load from a dialog box.

4.2.2. Commands for File-based Programming

To open a new file for typing procedure definitions, choose **NewFile** from the **File** menu. To edit an existing file, choose **EditFile**. As you type definitions into the file window, you evaluate them by selecting them with the mouse and choosing **Run Selection** from the **Logo** menu. To save the file on disk, choose either **Save File** or **Save File As...** from the **File** menu. Once you have saved a file, you can load it into workspace with the **Load...** and open it for editing with **EditFile**.

4.2.3. Advanced Use of Files

Object Logo includes an extensive repertoire for managing input and output to disk files. For example, you can write Logo procedures that read data from files, manipulate the data, and write new files using the results, or modify files that already exist. You can also rename, copy, move, and delete files from within Logo, rather than using the Macintosh Finder. See the Object Logo Manual for further information.

4.3. Aids for Debugging

One of the main features of Logo as a computer language for education is that students *design* and *write* programs as well as use them. *Debugging* a program is a crucial part of the programming process. This section describes some features included in the Logo system to aid in debugging programs.

4.3.1. STEP

Stepping causes procedures to be evaluated line-by-line "in slow motion." When a stepped procedure is called, Logo prints information about its inputs and outputs, and, before each line of the procedure is actually evaluated, Logo prints the line and waits for you to type a character before continuing.

Consider for example the **FLAG** and **RECTANGLE** procedures from section 2.1.2:

```
TO RECTANGLE :HEIGHT :LENGTH
FORWARD :HEIGHT
RIGHT 90
FORWARD :LENGTH
RIGHT 90
FORWARD :HEIGHT
RIGHT 90
FORWARD :LENGTH
RIGHT 90
END

TO FLAG :HEIGHT
FORWARD :HEIGHT
RECTANGLE (:HEIGHT / 2) :HEIGHT
BACK :HEIGHT
END
```

Here is how you can observe the turtle drawing a flag of size 50, step by step:

STEP [FLAG RECTANGLE]

```
FLAG 50
Entering FLAG with inputs: 50
FORWARD :HEIGHT                    ;you type a space after each of
                                   ;these lines
RECTANGLE (:HEIGHT / 2) :HEIGHT
 Entering RECTANGLE with inputs: 25 50
 FORWARD :HEIGHT
 RIGHT 90
 FORWARD :LENGTH
 RIGHT 90
 FORWARD :HEIGHT
 RIGHT 90
 FORWARD :LENGTH
 RIGHT 90
 Exiting RECTANGLE
BACK :HEIGHT
Exiting FLAG
```

Every time that either **FLAG** or **RECTANGLE** is evaluated, it will be stepped in this way. You can turn off stepping for a procedure by using the command **UNSTEP**. The **STEPPEDPROCS** command outputs a list of all the procedures that are currently being stepped.

4.3.2. TRACE

TRACE is similar to **STEP**, except that it just shows the inputs and outputs of the procedures, rather than stopping and waiting before the evaluation of each line. For instance, suppose you define the following three procedures to compute the average of a number and the cube of that number:[1]

---

[1] The **OUTPUT** command is discussed in section 5.2.

```
TO CUBE :X
OUTPUT :X * :X * :X
END

TO AVERAGE :X :Y
OUTPUT (:X + :Y) / 2
END

TO AV.WITH.CUBE :X
OUTPUT AVERAGE (CUBE :X) :X
END
```

Now you can trace the procedures to see how the inputs and outputs are passed among them:

TRACE [CUBE AVERAGE AV.WITH.CUBE]

Calling **AV.WITH.CUBE** with an input of 2 will cause **CUBE** to be called with an input of 2, so **CUBE** will output 8. **AVERAGE** will then be called with inputs of 8 and 2, and will output 5, which is finally output by **AV.WITH.CUBE**:

```
PRINT AV.WITH.CUBE 2
Entering AV.WITH.CUBE with inputs: 2
 Entering CUBE with inputs: 2
 Exiting CUBE with output: 8
 Entering AVERAGE with inputs: 8 2
 Exiting AVERAGE with output: 5
Exiting AV.WITH.CUBE with output: 5
5
```

UNTRACE will turn off tracing for procedures, and **TRACEDPROCS** returns a list of all traced procedures.

Bear in mind that **STEP** and **TRACE** are ordinary Logo commands that can be used inside procedures just like any other command. For example, suppose you are debugging a complicated program, and you wish to **STEP** a particular procedure, say **PROC**, only if some condition is true, say, only if **X** is less than 0. You can edit the part of the program that calls **PROC** to include the line

IF :X = 0 [STEP [PROC]]

before the call to **PROC**.

4.3.3. Watching Variable Values

Another useful Object Logo debugging feature gives you the ability to "watch" certain variables to see how their values change. The names are displayed along with their values in a *Watch* window, and the values are updated as they change. For example, suppose you write a program to model deposits to a bank account:

```
MAKE "TOTAL 0
MAKE "DEPOSIT 0
MAKE "NUM_DEPOSITS 0

TO DEPOSIT :D
MAKE "DEPOSIT :D
MAKE "NUM_DEPOSITS :NUM_DEPOSITS + 1
MAKE "TOTAL :TOTAL + :DEPOSIT
END
```

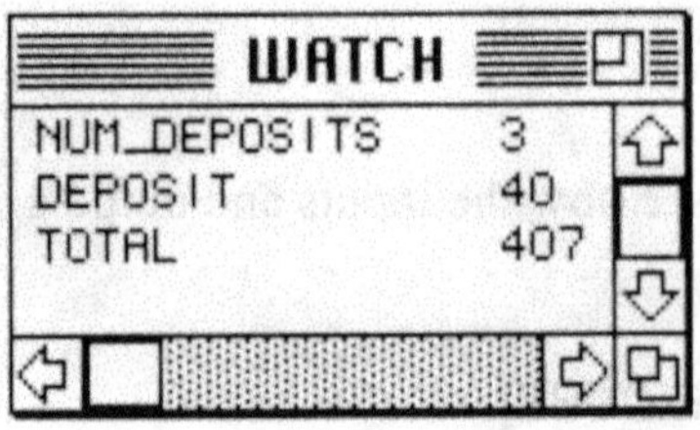

You can use the **WATCH** command to see how the total amount, current deposit, and number of deposits change as you make deposits:

WATCH [TOTAL DEPOSIT NUM_DEPOSITS]

Figure 4.1 shows how the Watch window appears after you evaluate

DEPOSIT 100
DEPOSIT 267
DEPOSIT 40

Figure 4.1: Using the Watch window to observe changing values of variables

To turn off watching for a variable, use the **UNWATCH** command. **WATCHEDNAMES** returns the list of all names currently being watched.

4.3.4. PAUSE and DEBUG

The **PAUSE** command enables you to pause evaluation of a program to perform various debugging activities (for example to examine the values of variables at some intermediate point in a program) and then resume running the program.

As an example of how **PAUSE** is used, consider the **FLAG** and **RECTANGLE** procedures in section 4.3.1, where **FLAG** has been edited to insert pauses before and after the call to **RECTANGLE**. The input words to **PAUSE** are messages that Logo will print when the pauses occur.[2]

```
TO FLAG :HEIGHT
FORWARD :HEIGHT
(PAUSE "BEFORE.RECT)
RECTANGLE (:HEIGHT / 2) :HEIGHT
(PAUSE "AFTER.RECT)
BACK :HEIGHT
END
```

---

[2] The **PAUSE** command and the input word are enclosed in parentheses. This is because the input word is an *optional input* to the **PAUSE** command. If you do not specify an input word, then Logo will pause without printing any message. Using parentheses with optional inputs is explained in section 5.7.2.

You see the pauses happen when you evaluate **FLAG 50**. The following example shows how you can examine the turtle's position before and after drawing the rectangle:

```
? FLAG 50
BEFORE.RECT
    ? PRINT POS          ;the prompt is indented at a pause
0. 50.
    ? CONTINUE
AFTER.RECT
    ? PRINT POS
0. 50.
    ? CONTINUE
?
```

Notice how at a pause, the Logo question mark prompt is indented. The **CONTINUE** command makes Logo continues evaluation after a pause. If you want to stop evaluation of the program immediately and return to top level, use the command **TOPLEVEL**.

If you give the command **DEBUG** (or select **Debug** from the **Logo** menu), Logo will enter a state where it will pause, on any error, rather than just returning to top level as usual. The **NODEBUG** command turns this behavior off. Also, typing **Command-,** (or selecting **Pause** from the **Logo** menu) during evaluation of a program, will cause Logo to pause.

CHAPTER **5**

Numbers, Words, and Lists

In the previous chapters, we used turtle geometry to introduce the basic techniques for writing Logo procedures. We now move away from graphics to discuss Logo programs that work with "data." Like most computer languages, Logo provides operations for manipulating numbers and character strings, which in Logo are called *words*. One significant difference between Logo and other simple programming languages is that Logo also provides the ability to combine data into structures called *lists*. This chapter introduces these three kinds of data objects—numbers, words, and lists—together with simple programs that manipulate them. The most important concept in working with Logo data is the notion of a procedure that *outputs a value*. This is introduced in section 5.2 below. We also discuss the use of Logo variables for naming data, and we give a more complete explanation of testing and conditionals than the one provided in section 2.2.2. The material presented here provides enough background to complete many programming projects, such as the ones described in Chapter 6.

5.1. Numbers and Arithmetic

We have already seen examples of using numbers in turtle programs. Logo provides the basic arithmetic operations of addition, subtraction, multiplication, and division, denoted by **+, −, ***, and **/**, respectively. In combining arithmetic operations, multiplications and divisions are performed before additions and subtractions unless you use parentheses to make the grouping explicit. Here are some examples.

PRINT 3 + 2 * 5
13

PRINT (3 + 2) * 5
25

The result of an operation is normally used as an input to a command like **PRINT** or **FORWARD**, or a procedure like **POLY**. If you do not supply a command to accept the result of an operation Logo will print an error message:

(3 + 2) * 5
You don't say what to do with 25.

5.1.1. Real Numbers

Logo also allows numbers that include a decimal part. These are often called *real numbers* in computer jargon. Here are some examples of real numbers:

| 4.56 | 3.10 | .00750 | .0075 |
| 12.345 | 3.21 | −2.59 | −.123 |

If you type a real number that has no fractional part after the decimal point, **Object Logo will treat that as an integer:**

PRINT 5.
5
PRINT 5.0
5

Integers and real numbers may be mixed freely in arithmetic operations, for example:

PRINT 3.96 − 12
−8.04

Exponential notation

Logo allows you to indicate real numbers in *exponential notation*. Here are some examples:

| 3E4 | 5N2 | −4E4 | −4N5 |
| 3.4E4 | 4.56N3 | −2.5925E5 | −259.3N7 |

Exponential notation is of the form:

{number} {**E** or **N**} {exponent}

where {number} (also called the *mantissa*) is either an integer or a real number written in standard decimal form and {exponent} is a positive integer. If the letter is **E** then the resulting real number is interpreted as {mantissa}$*10^{\{exponent\}}$. If the letter is **N** then the resulting real number is interpreted as {mantissa}$*10^{-\{exponent\}}$. For example, **5.2E3** is the same as **5200.0** and **5.2N3** is the same as **.0052**. The following are not in correct form:

3E5.1	the exponent is not an integer
2.7E−1	use **N** for 10 to a negative power
10 E1	there should be no space between the **10** and the **E**
E1	there must be a mantissa

Real numbers must be between -10^{308} and 10^{308}. Integers can be arbitrarily large.

5.1.2. Ratios

In addition to integers and real numbers, Object Logo also provides *ratios*. A ratio is the result of dividing two integers. When you divide two integers, Object Logo will produce either a whole number or a ratio reduced to lowest terms, depending on whether the answer comes out evenly:

```
PRINT 10 / 4
5/2
PRINT 10 / 5
2
PRINT 5 / 2
5 / 2
```

In general, you need not worry about whether you are performing arithmetic operations with integers, real numbers, or ratios, because Object Logo will automatically convert between them. The result of any arithmetic operation will be returned in "simplest form," where an integer is considered to be simpler than a ratio, which is considered to be simpler than a real number. This is shown in the following examples:

```
PRINT 5 + 2.7
7.7
PRINT 5 + 11 / 3
26/3
PRINT 5.7 + 11 / 3
9.366666666666667
PRINT 1 / 3 + 11 / 3
4
```

5.1.3. Numeric Operations

Object Logo provides an extensive collection of numeric operations, including exponentials, logarithms, and trigonometric functions. There are also complex numbers, whose real and imaginary parts can be integers, real numbers, or ratios. Refer to the Object Logo manual for complete information on these operations. Here are some examples:

```
PRINT ROUND 2.7          ;round 2.7 to an integer
3
PRINT REMAINDER 29 3     ;remainder of 29 divided by 3
2
PRINT POWER 2 10         ;2 raised to the 10th power
1024
PRINT SQRT 2             ;square root of 2
1.414213562373095
PRINT LOG 32 2           ;log of 32 to the base 2
5.
PRINT COS 60             ;cosine of 60 degrees
0.5
PRINT SQRT –100          ;square root of –100
0+10i
```

Random numbers

RANDOM is an operation that takes a positive number n as input and outputs an integer chosen at random from 0 up to, but not including, the integer part of n. Thus **RANDOM 2** will output either 0 or 1, and **RANDOM 999.5** will output an integer less than 1000.

Each time Object Logo is started, successive calls to **RANDOM** with identical inputs yield the identical sequence of random numbers. The sequence of random numbers is also restarted if you give the command **RERANDOM**. This is useful for debugging programs that use **RANDOM**, since you can be sure that **RANDOM** will return the same sequence each time you try the program.

Suppose, however, you are running a demonstration program that uses **RANDOM**, and you would like the program to do something different each time Logo is started. You can make this happen by calling the following **RANDOMIZE** procedure when you start Logo:

```
TO RANDOMIZE
MAKE "X RANDOM 10000
IF KEYP [STOP]
RANDOMIZE
END
```

RANDOMIZE keeps generating random numbers until you stop it by pressing a key (tested for by the **KEYP** primitive). Since you won't wait *exactly* the same amount of time each time you use **RANDOMIZE**, the random number generator will be left in a different state each time.

5.2. Outputs

Using the arithmetic operations presented above, you can write procedures that manipulate numbers. For example,

```
TO PSQUARE :X
PRINT :X * :X
END
```

prints the square of its input, and

```
TO PAVERAGE :X :Y
PRINT (:X + :Y) * .5
END
```

prints the average of its two inputs:

```
PSQUARE 100
10000
PAVERAGE 1 2
1.5
```

These procedures may be instructive, but they are not very useful. **PSQUARE**, for example, just prints the square of its input. Having computed the square, there is nothing more you can do with it. Yet the whole power of the procedure concept is that you should be able to use procedures as *building blocks* in defining more complex procedures. You can make complex turtle programs by combining the designs drawn by simple procedures. But there is no way to combine **PSQUARE** and **PAVERAGE** to obtain, for instance, the square of the average of two numbers.

What is needed is some way for a procedure not only to compute some result, but also to make that result accessible to other procedures. In Logo, this is accomplished by the **OUTPUT** command. To see how it works, compare the **PSQUARE** procedure above with the following:

```
TO SQUARE :X
OUTPUT :X * :X
END
```

When **SQUARE** runs, it returns its result as an *output* that is used as an input to whatever procedure called **SQUARE**. For example, you can type

```
PRINT SQUARE 3
9
```

in which case the output of **SQUARE** is passed to **PRINT** to be printed. More significantly, you could type

```
PRINT (SQUARE 3) + (SQUARE 4)
25
```

Here **SQUARE** is called twice, and the results are combined by **+** before being passed to **PRINT**.

You can do the same thing with computing averages by defining a procedure:

```
TO AVERAGE :X :Y
OUTPUT (:X + :Y) * .5
END
```

The **OUTPUT** command is just what is needed to combine operations. For instance, you can find the square of the average of two numbers:

```
PRINT SQUARE (AVERAGE 5 6)
30.25
```

or the average of the squares:

```
PRINT AVERAGE (SQUARE 5) (SQUARE 6)
30.5
```

Alternatively, you can define a procedure to return this value to be used in further processing:

```
TO AVERAGE.OF.SQUARES :X :Y
OUTPUT AVERAGE (SQUARE :X) (SQUARE :Y)
END
```

As with any procedure, once you have defined a procedure that outputs some result, that procedure becomes part of Logo's working vocabulary and can be used just as if it were a primitive command. For instance, the following **LIMIT** function limits **X** to be between **A** and **B**, that is, it outputs **A** if **X** is less than **A**, it outputs **B** if **X** is greater **B**, and it outputs **X** if **X** is between **A** and **B**:

```
TO LIMIT :X :A :B
IF :X < :A [OUTPUT :A]
IF :X > :B [OUTPUT :B]
OUTPUT :X
END
```

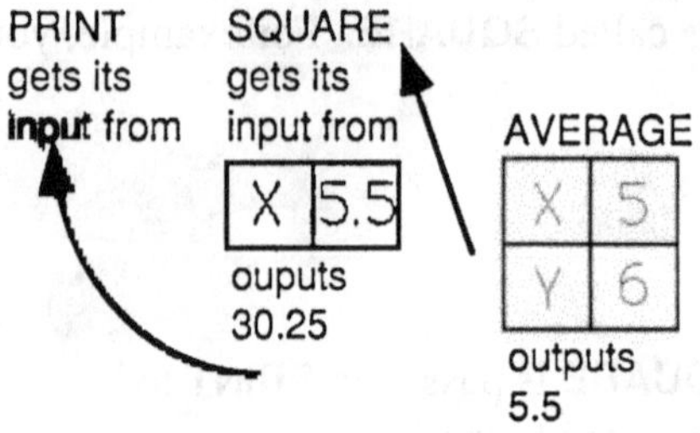

You can use this **LIMIT** operation in performing further computations, just as if it were a Logo primitive.

When a procedure evaluates an **OUTPUT** instruction, it returns the indicated output to the procedure that called it, and no further commands within the procedure are evaluated. Thus, for example, precisely one of the three **OUTPUT** instructions in **LIMIT** will be evaluated each time **LIMIT** is called.

To help you visualize outputs, figure 5.1 shows a diagram, similar to the diagrams in section 2.1.2, for the procedure calls involved in evaluating the command

PRINT SQUARE (AVERAGE 5 6)

SQUARE and **AVERAGE** each have a private variable **X**, but since these are in different private libraries, there is no conflict.

As shown in the diagram, you can regard inputs and outputs as communication channels between procedures. If procedure A calls procedure B, then A can use inputs to communicate values to B. B's output enables it to communicate values back to A.

Figure 5.1: Procedure calls in evaluating **PRINT SQUARE (AVERAGE 5 6)**

5.3. Words

In Logo, strings of characters are called *words*. Logo provides operations for manipulating words: combining words into longer words and breaking words into parts. As with numbers, words maybe passed among procedures as inputs and outputs.

To indicate a word in Logo, you type the character string prefixed by a quotation mark, as in

PRINT "WHOOPIE
WHOOPIE

Notice that (unlike the rule in English) the quotation mark goes only at the beginning of the word. Beware that if you put a quotation mark at the end of a word, that quotation mark will be taken to be part of the word:

PRINT "A"
A"

Logo supplies the following operations for extracting parts of words:

FIRST	Outputs the first character of its word input.
LAST	Outputs the last character.
BUTFIRST	Outputs a word containing all but the first character. Abbreviated **BF**.
BUTLAST	Outputs a word containing all but the last character. Abbreviated **BL**.

Here are some examples:

PRINT FIRST "ABCD
A

PRINT BUTFIRST "ABCD
BCD

PRINT LAST BUTLAST "ABCD
C

PRINT BUTFIRST "A
(blank line)

In the third example, the thing that is printed is the **LAST** of the **BUTLAST** of **ABCD** which is the **LAST** of **ABC** which is **C**.

Note that in the last example **BUTLAST** outputs all but the first character of the one-character word **A**. The result is a word containing *no* characters. This no-character word is called the *empty word*. According to the rule for inputting words, you can specify the empty word by typing a quotation mark followed by *no* characters:

PRINT "
(blank line)

Attempting to extract **FIRST, BUTFIRST, LAST,** or **BUTLAST** of the empty word causes Logo to signal an error.

For constructing larger words from smaller ones, Logo provides the **WORD** operation. This takes two words as inputs and combines them to form a single word:

PRINT WORD "NOW "HERE
NOWHERE

Numbers are considered to be Logo words, and all word-manipulating operations work on numbers:

PRINT FIRST 4567
4

```
PRINT BUTFIRST 4567
567

PRINT (WORD 12  34) + (WORD 56  78)
6912
```

Sample procedures that use words

The following recursive procedure is a word analogue of the **COUNTDOWN** procedure in chapter 2.

```
TO TRIANGLE :WORD
IF :WORD = "  [STOP]
PRINT :WORD
TRIANGLE BUTFIRST :WORD
END

TRIANGLE "LOLLIPOP
LOLLIPOP
OLLIPOP
LLIPOP
LIPOP
IPOP
POP
OP
P
```

Whereas **COUNTDOWN** reduced a number to smaller numbers by successively subtracting 1, **TRIANGLE** reduces a word to smaller words by successively removing the first character. The process stops when the word has been reduced to the empty word.

TRIANGLE illustrates the use of words as inputs to procedures. As an example of words as outputs, consider the simple procedure **DOUBLE**, which takes a word as input and outputs the word concatenated with itself:

```
TO DOUBLE :X
OUTPUT WORD :X :X
END

PRINT DOUBLE "BOOM
BOOMBOOM
```

Observe the importance of using **OUTPUT**: you can operate on a word using **DOUBLE** and use the result as an input to other operations:

```
PRINT DOUBLE DOUBLE "BOOM
BOOMBOOMBOOMBOOM
```

```
TRIANGLE DOUBLE "ABC
ABCABC
BCABC
CABC
ABC
BC
C
```

Special characters in words

When you type a word by beginning with a quotation mark, the word will be taken to be all the characters following the quotation mark up to a space, the end of the line, or one of several special characters:

```
+ – * / ^ = < > ( ) [ ] ;
```

However, if one of the above characters appears immediately following a quotation mark, then it is taken as the first character of the quoted word.

In Object Logo, if you want to include spaces or special characters in a word, use a vertical bar (|) as the first and last character of the word. The word will consist of all the characters between the vertical bars, not including the bars.

```
PRINT "|HELLO THERE (THIS IS A STRANGE WORD)|
HELLO THERE (THIS IS A STRANGE WORD)
```

5.4. Lists

Many languages force the programmer to work with text in terms of character strings. A long text must be viewed as a long character string that is manipulated on a character by character basis. One of the advantages of Logo is that it allows you to manipulate sequences of words on a *word by word* basis. In Logo, a sequence of words is called a *list*. A list may be indicated by giving the words in the list separated by spaces and enclosed in square brackets:[1]

```
PRINT [THIS IS A LIST]
THIS IS A LIST
```

Notice that the words in the list are not quoted and that the surrounding brackets are not printed. If you want to see the outer brackets, use the command **SHOW** instead of **PRINT**:

```
SHOW  [THIS IS A LIST]
[THIS IS A LIST]
```

---

[1] Logo lists are used not only for making sequences of words, but also for creating data structures in general. See section 10.1. Remember to delimit lists with square brackets [ ] and not parentheses ( ).

Spaces between words in lists serve only to delimit the words. Extra spaces are ignored:

PRINT [EXTRA   SPACES]
EXTRA SPACES

The Logo operations **FIRST, LAST, BUTFIRST,** and **BUTLAST** that we introduced for use with words also operate on lists. When used with lists, these operations pick out the first or last word of the list, rather than the first or last character, as they do with words.

PRINT FIRST [THIS IS A LIST]
THIS

PRINT FIRST BUTFIRST [THIS IS A LIST]
IS

PRINT BUTLAST [THIS IS STILL A LIST]
THIS IS STILL A

PRINT BUTFIRST [THIS]
(blank line)

SHOW BUTFIRST [THIS]
[ ]

Note that in the last example, taking all but the first word of a list that has only one word produces a list containing *no* words, called the *empty list*. It can be typed into Logo as **[ ]**. The empty list is analogous to the empty word, but they are not the same thing. This is a special case of the rule that a list in Logo is never considered equal to a word. Another case of the same rule is that a word is not considered equal to a list that contains that single word, even though Logo prints these in the same way:

PRINT "BUBBLE
BUBBLE

PRINT [BUBBLE]
BUBBLE

PRINT "BUBBLE = [BUBBLE]
FALSE

SENTENCE is the operation for putting lists together, analogous to **WORD** for words. **SENTENCE** (abbreviated **SE**) takes two words or lists as inputs and assembles these into one list:

PRINT SENTENCE [THIS IS] [HOW SENTENCE WORKS]
THIS IS HOW SENTENCE WORKS

```
PRINT SENTENCE "THIS [IS TOO]
THIS IS TOO

PRINT SENTENCE "THIS "ALSO
THIS ALSO
```

Sample procedures that use lists

Here are the list procedures analogous to the word procedures **TRIANGLE** and **DOUBLE** of section 5.3:

```
TO TRIANGLE.LIST :X
IF :X = [ ] [STOP]
PRINT :X
TRIANGLE.LIST BUTFIRST :X
END


TO DOUBLE.LIST :X
OUTPUT SENTENCE :X :X
END


TRIANGLE.LIST [THIS IS A LIST]
THIS IS A LIST
IS A LIST
A LIST
LIST


PRINT DOUBLE.LIST [HUP 2 3 4]
HUP 2 3 4 HUP 2 3 4


TRIANGLE.LIST DOUBLE.LIST [DING DONG]
DING DONG DING DONG
DONG DING DONG
DING DONG
DONG
```

The main thing to observe in these examples is that lists, like numbers and words, can be passed between procedures as inputs and outputs.

The following list procedures make use of the Logo command **READLIST,** which makes it easy to write interactive programs using lists. **READLIST** waits for you to type in a line (terminated by RETURN) and outputs the typed-in line as a list.

```
TO BOAST
PRINT [WHO'S THE GREATEST?]
IF READLIST = [ME] [PRINT [OF COURSE!] STOP]
PRINT [NO, TRY AGAIN]
BOAST
END


BOAST
WHO'S THE GREATEST?
```

MIGHTY MOUSE
NO, TRY AGAIN
WHO'S THE GREATEST?
ME
OF COURSE!

Bear in mind that **READLIST** always outputs a list. If you type in a single word, the output of **READLIST** will be a list containing that one word. If you just press RETURN without typing anything, the output of **READLIST** will be the empty list.
Here's another example:

TO CHAT
PRINT [WHAT'S YOUR NAME?]
PRINT SENTENCE [HELLO] READLIST
PRINT [TYPE SOMETHING YOU LIKE]
PRINT SENTENCE [I'M GLAD YOU LIKE] READLIST
END

Notice how the second line of the procedure is constructed: the list being **PRINT**ed is a **SENTENCE** of two things—the list **[HELLO]** and the list output by **READLIST**.

CHAT
WHAT'S YOUR NAME?
LUCY
HELLO LUCY
TYPE SOMETHING YOU LIKE
PICKLE JELLO
I'M GLAD YOU LIKE PICKLE JELLO

5.5. Naming

We have so far seen two different kinds of *naming* in Logo programs: the use of names to refer to inputs to procedures, and the idea of naming procedures themselves. But we have not yet seen Logo programs in which names are given freely to data.

The Logo command used to name things is **MAKE**. Consider the following:

MAKE "NUMBER 5
PRINT :NUMBER
5

In the first line you tell Logo that you are going to call the number 5 by the name **NUMBER**. The first input to **MAKE** is the *name* and the second input is the *thing* you are naming. The effect of the command is to establish a relationship between the word **NUMBER** and the number 5. We express this by saying that "5 is the thing associated with **NUMBER**." In the line

PRINT :NUMBER

you can see how : recovers the thing associated with the name, just as it recovers the value associated with an input to a procedure. Here are more examples:

MAKE "COLR "YELLOW
PRINT "COLR
COLR

PRINT :COLR
YELLOW

MAKE "SLOGAN [I LOVE BANANAS]
PRINT :SLOGAN
I LOVE BANANAS

PRINT SENTENCE (BUTLAST :SLOGAN) :COLR
I LOVE YELLOW

In these examples, and in most programs, the name is specified as a literal, quoted word. This is not the only possibility:

MAKE (WORD "PART 1) [DO MI SOL]
PRINT :PART1
DO MI SOL

Here is a tricky example:

MAKE "FLOWER "ROSE
PRINT :FLOWER
ROSE

MAKE :FLOWER [IS A ROSE IS A ROSE]
PRINT :FLOWER
ROSE

PRINT :ROSE
IS A ROSE IS A ROSE

In the third command line, the name associated with **[IS A ROSE IS A ROSE]** is not the literal word **FLOWER**, but rather the *thing* associated with **FLOWER**, that is, the word **ROSE**. Therefore

MAKE :FLOWER {something}

has the same effect as

MAKE "ROSE {something}

The Logo function **THING** returns the thing associated with its input. The use of **:** is actually an abbreviation for **THING** in the case where the input to **THING** is a quoted literal word. But **THING** can be used in more general circumstances:

MAKE "NAME1 [JOHN Q. CITIZEN]
PRINT :NAME1
JOHN Q. CITIZEN

PRINT THING "NAME1
JOHN Q. CITIZEN

PRINT THING (WORD "NA "ME1)
JOHN Q. CITIZEN

PRINT THING (FIRST [NAME1 PLACE1])
JOHN Q. CITIZEN

There is also the Logo predicate **NAMEP,** which takes a word as input and outputs **TRUE** if the word is the name of a Logo thing.

5.5.1. Local and Global Names

In section 2.1.2 we saw that the names of inputs are *private* to the procedures using them. Different procedures reference names in different private libraries, and two procedures may use the same names for different purposes without any conflict. The same holds true if the procedure uses the **MAKE** command to change the value associated with some input name. This is illustrated in the following example:

TO DEMO :X
PRINT :X
CHANGE :X
PRINT :X
END

TO CHANGE :X
MAKE "X :X + 1
PRINT :X
END

DEMO 1
1   (printed in **DEMO**)
2   (printed in **CHANGE**)
1   (printed in **DEMO**)

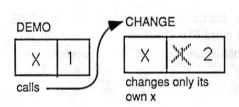

DEMO   CHANGE

X | 1   X | X 2

calls   changes only its own x

Figure 5.2: Private libraries for **DEMO** and **CHANGE**

The important point to notice is that when the value of **X** is printed in **DEMO** the second time, it is still 1 even though **CHANGE** "changed" **X** to 2. The reason is that **DEMO** and **CHANGE** each have their own meaning for **X** in different private libraries, as shown in figure 5.2. When **CHANGE** uses the **MAKE** statement it changes *its* **X**, but not **DEMO**'s.

When you use a **MAKE** statement at toplevel, you are also associating a value with a name in some library. But this is not a library associated with any procedure. Rather it is a library associated with the command level. Definitions in this library are sometimes called *global variables*. Just as the private libraries of two procedures are distinct, names in procedure libraries will not conflict with names in the global library. Compare the following example to the one above.

```
MAKE "X 1
CHANGE :X
2
PRINT :X
1
```

Local variables

It is sometimes useful to have private variables for a procedure, in addition to the procedure's inputs. You do this with the **LOCAL** command, which takes as input a list of variables to be made local to the procedure. In the following example, **DISTANCE** uses local variables **DX** and **DY**:

```
TO DISTANCE :X1 :Y1 :X2 :Y2
LOCAL [DX DY]
MAKE "DX :X1 – :X2
MAKE "DY :Y1 – :Y2
OUTPUT SQRT (:DX * :DX) + (:DY * :DY)
END
```

```
PRINT DISTANCE 0  0  20  30
36.0555
```

DISTANCE would still work here without the **LOCAL** declaration, but the two **MAKE** commands would define **DX** and **DY** as global variables.

5.5.2. Free Variables

One of the reasons that procedures are so important is that they provide a way to design complex programs in small pieces. But whenever you design something by breaking it into pieces, you eventually have to deal with the issue of how these pieces can interact. The importance of the private library mechanism is that it guarantees that the names used by different procedures will refer to different things and hence that the *only* way procedures can interact is through inputs and outputs. This guarantee provides a good handle on controlling the complexity of the entire program.

Sometimes, however, it is convenient for procedures to interact other than through inputs and outputs. For example, if the computation performed by a procedure depends on a large number of parameters, it may be cumbersome to specify them all as inputs each time the procedure is called. Again, using only inputs and outputs to pass information may require passing "superfluous" inputs through many levels of nested procedures until they reach the procedure that actually needs them. For these reasons it is useful to be able to have the computation performed by a procedure depend not only on the information provided *explicitly* by the inputs, but also on information that is *implicit* to the *context* in which the procedure is used.

Consider the following procedure:

```
TO NEW.PRICE :P
OUTPUT :P + :OVERHEAD
END
```

The value returned by **NEW.PRICE** depends not only upon the input **P**, but also upon some **OVERHEAD** that is obtained from the context in which the procedure is used. Here is an example:

```
MAKE "OVERHEAD 50
PRINT NEW.PRICE 100
150
```

```
MAKE "OVERHEAD 25
PRINT NEW.PRICE 100
125
```

The name **OVERHEAD** in the **NEW.PRICE** procedure illustrates what is known in computer-science jargon as a *free variable*. A free variable is a variable that is referenced in a procedure, but is not local to the procedure. In the example, **OVERHEAD** is a free variable that refers to the global library.

Procedures can change, the value of free variables as well as reference them, as shown by the following example:

```
TO INCREASE.COSTS
MAKE "OVERHEAD :OVERHEAD + 1
END
```

```
MAKE "OVERHEAD 25
PRINT :OVERHEAD
25
```

```
INCREASE.COSTS
PRINT :OVERHEAD
26
PRINT NEW.PRICE 100
126
```

Public variables

Free variables in a procedure need not necessarily refer to the global library. Another possibility is that the free variable is determined by a procedure that calls the given procedure. Object Logo refers to such variables as *public variables*. Here is an example:

```
TO TRY.COST :OVERHEAD
PUBLIC [OVERHEAD]
PRINT NEW.PRICE 100
END
```

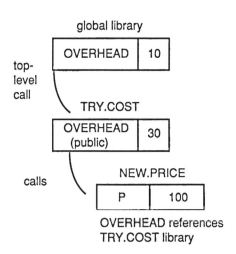

Figure 5.3: Private libraries when **NEW.PRICE** is called by **TRY.COST**

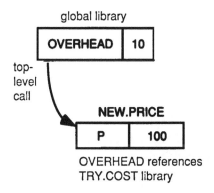

Figure 5.4: Private libraries when **NEW.PRICE** is called from top level.

MAKE "OVERHEAD 10
TRY.COST 30
130
PRINT NEW.PRICE 100
110

The line

PUBLIC [OVERHEAD]

in the **TRY.COST** procedure declares that **OVERHEAD** should be a public variable. This means that **OVERHEAD** will be seen by any procedure that **TRY.COST** calls, or any procedures called by those procedures, and so on.

Figures 5.3 and 5.4 show the private libraries for the procedures in the above example. When **NEW.PRICE** is called by **TRY.COST**, its free variable **OVERHEAD** references the public **OVERHEAD** variable in the library for **TRY.COST** (whose value is 30). When **NEW.PRICE** is called directly from top level, its free variable **OVERHEAD** references the **OVERHEAD** in the global library (whose value is 10).

The presence of public variables leads to the following rule for referencing variable names in Logo procedures:

- If the name is the name of an input to the procedure, the reference is in the procedure's private library.

- Otherwise, see if the name is a public variable in the library of a procedure that *called* the current procedure.

- Otherwise, see if the name is a public variable in the procedure that called *that* procedure, and so on, all the way through to the global library.

Public variables provide a powerful mechanism for passing information between procedures. But their indiscriminate use leads to obscure programs and may result in intractable program bugs. The is especially true if you use **MAKE** to change the value of a free variable, since the actual variable affected may appear arbitrarily far back in the chain of procedure calls.[2]

Bear in mind that if you do not explicitly declare a variable in a procedure to be public, it will *not* be seen by called procedures. The following example is similar to **TRY.COST** above, except that the **OVERHEAD** variable is not declared public. Therefore both calls to **NEW.PRICE** reference the **OVERHEAD** in the global library:

---

[2] Object Logo's public variables are more traditionally known as *dynamically-bound variables* in computer-science jargon.

```
TO TRY.COST1 :OVERHEAD
PRINT NEW.PRICE 100
END

MAKE "OVERHEAD 10
TRY.COST1 30
110
PRINT NEW.PRICE 100
110
```

5.6. Conditional Expressions and Predicates

We saw in section 2.2.2 the use of conditional expressions **IF** ... in Logo programs. This section provides more information about conditional expressions.

The general form of an **IF** statement is

IF some condition [action]

For example, the following procedure tells whether a number is positive or negative:

```
TO SIGN :N
IF :N < 0 [OUTPUT "NEGATIVE]
IF :N > 0 [OUTPUT "POSITIVE]
END

PRINT SIGN 57
POSITIVE
PRINT SIGN (10 – 20)
NEGATIVE
```

IF expressions are often confusing for beginning programmers, due to the need to work with a single statement that specifies both a test and the action to be taken depending on the outcome of the test. Logo therefore includes another form of conditional that separates the testing from the actions. This form is **TEST** ... **IFTRUE** ... **IFFALSE**. The **TEST** used in a procedure checks some condition. Subsequent procedure lines that begin with **IFTRUE** and **IFFALSE** are evaluated or not depending on the result of the **TEST**. Here's another way to write the **SIGN** procedure using **TEST**:

```
TO SIGN :N
TEST :N < 0
IFTRUE [OUTPUT "NEGATIVE]
IFFALSE [OUTPUT "POSITIVE ]
END
```

A procedure can include more than one **TEST**, and any **IFTRUE** or **IFFALSE** statements always refer to the most recent **TEST**. Also, the result of a **TEST** is kept private within a procedure, so the use of **IFTRUE** and **IFFALSE** within a procedure is not affected by any **TEST**s performed in a subprocedure.

Predicates; the words TRUE and FALSE

The conditions checked by **IF** and **TEST** are known as *predicates*. We already introduced the Logo predicates >, <, and = for working with numbers. It is easy to define new predicates, because a predicate in Logo is nothing more than a procedure that outputs either the word **TRUE** or the word **FALSE**. For instance, you can transform the **SIGN** procedure given above into a predicate that outputs **FALSE** if the input is less than 0 and **TRUE** otherwise:[3]

```
TO POSITIVE? :X
IF :X < 0 [OUTPUT "FALSE]
OUTPUT "TRUE
END
```

As another example, the following predicate takes a word as input and tests whether it begins with a vowel:

```
TO BEGINS.WITH.VOWEL? :X
IF (FIRST :X) = "A [OUTPUT "TRUE]
IF (FIRST :X) = "E [OUTPUT "TRUE]
IF (FIRST :X) = "I [OUTPUT "TRUE]
IF (FIRST :X) = "O [OUTPUT "TRUE]
IF (FIRST :X) = "U [OUTPUT "TRUE]
OUTPUT "FALSE
END
```

Once a predicate has been defined, it can be used with **IF** or **TEST** just as if it were one of the predicates built in to Logo. Here is a procedure that adds "a" or "an" to a word, as appropriate:[4]

```
TO ADD.A.OR.AN :X
TEST BEGINS.WITH.VOWEL? :X
IFTRUE [OUTPUT SENTENCE "AN :X]
IFFALSE [OUTPUT SENTENCE "A :X]
END
```

```
PRINT ADD.A.OR.AN "COMPUTER
A COMPUTER
PRINT ADD.A.OR.AN "APPLE
AN APPLE
```

You can regard **IF** and **TEST** as operations that take an input that must be either the word **TRUE** or the word **FALSE**. In fact, the primitive predicates built in to Logo are themselves are also operations that output **TRUE** or **FALSE**:

---

[3] It is a good programming habit to name predicates with names that end with a question mark or with the letter P (for "predicate"). Object Logo's built-in predicates tend to have names that end in P.

[4] Later on, when we see how to take advantage of Logo lists as data structures, we will learn more flexible ways to compute functions like **BEGINS.WITH.VOWEL?**. Compare the alternative version of the **ADD.A.OR.AN** procedure in section 10.3.2.

```
PRINT 3 > 5
FALSE
PRINT "XYZ = "XYZ
TRUE
```

For combining predicates, Logo includes the operation **AND**, which takes inputs that must be either **TRUE** or **FALSE**, and outputs **TRUE** if all inputs are **TRUE** and **FALSE** otherwise. There is also **OR**, which outputs **TRUE** if at least one of its inputs is **TRUE**, and **NOT**, which outputs **TRUE** if its input is **FALSE**, and **FALSE** if its input is true.

```
PRINT AND (1 < 2) (2 > 3)
FALSE
PRINT OR (1 < 2) (2 > 3)
TRUE
PRINT NOT (2 + 2 = 4)
FALSE
```

For example, here are three equivalent ways of writing a predicate **BETWEEN?**, which tests whether a specified number is in a given range:

```
TO BETWEEN? :X :LOW :HIGH
IF :X < :LOW [OUTPUT "FALSE]
IF :X > :HIGH [OUTPUT "FALSE]
OUTPUT "TRUE
END


TO BETWEEN? :X :LOW :HIGH
IF OR (:X < :LOW) (:X > :HIGH) [OUTPUT "FALSE]
OUTPUT "TRUE
END


TO BETWEEN? :X :LOW :HIGH
IF AND (NOT (:X < :LOW)) (NOT (:X > :HIGH))
_ [OUTPUT "TRUE]
OUTPUT "FALSE
END
```

AND and **OR** are themselves predicates that output **TRUE** or **FALSE**. This means that the second two versions of **BETWEEN?** can also be written in another way, in which the **TRUE** or **FALSE** output by **AND** and **OR** is output directly to the procedure that calls **BETWEEN?**:

```
TO BETWEEN? :X :LOW :HIGH
OUTPUT AND (NOT (:X < :LOW)) (NOT (:X > :HIGH))
END


TO BETWEEN? :X :LOW :HIGH
OUTPUT NOT OR (:X < :LOW) (:X > :HIGH)
END
```

5.7. Details on Logo Syntax

This section collects some information about how Logo interprets the command lines that you type to it. This includes such information as where to include spaces and parentheses in command lines, and how Logo groups sequences of commands.

5.7.1. How Logo Separates Lines into Words

Any Logo line is interpreted as a sequence of words. In general, you must separate words by spaces. For example, if you mean to type

FORWARD 100

and instead type

FORWARD100

Logo will respond with the error message

You haven't told me how to FORWARD100.

because it will interpret **FORWARD100** as a single word and look for a procedure with that name.[5] As a general rule, it is a good idea to type each line with spaces between the different elements, for example,

PRINT (3 + 4) * 5
35

Logo does, however, understand that parentheses and arithmetic operators are normally meant to break words, so

PRINT (3+4)*5
35

works, too.

5.7.2. Using Parentheses

We have already seen some complex Logo expressions, for example, the following line from the **AVERAGE.OF.SQUARES** procedure in section 5.2.

OUTPUT AVERAGE (SQUARE :X) (SQUARE :Y)

In this line, the **OUTPUT** command takes one input, which is the result of **AVERAGE**. **AVERAGE** in turn takes two inputs:

(SQUARE :X)

---

[5] Of course, you may have actually defined a procedure whose name was **FORWARD100**, in which case Logo would run that procedure.

and

(SQUARE :Y)

Notice that parentheses perform grouping by enclosing the operation *together with its inputs*. That is, you should write

(SQUARE :X)

and not

SQUARE (:X)

to indicate that **:X** is the input to **SQUARE**.[6]

In fact, this expression would work perfectly well if you wrote it without any parentheses at all, as

OUTPUT AVERAGE SQUARE :X SQUARE :Y

because when Logo interprets the line it breaks things up according to the following method. The first word it sees is **OUTPUT**, and this requires one input. So Logo scans the line trying to find that input. The next thing it runs into, though, is **AVERAGE**, which requires two inputs of its own. So Logo now scans to find two inputs for **AVER-AGE** and runs into **SQUARE**, which requires one input which Logo finds as **:X**. This completes the input to **SQUARE**, and also completes the first input to **AVERAGE**. Logo now looks for the second input to **AVERAGE**, and the next thing it sees is another **SQUARE**, which requires one input. Logo finds this as **:Y**. Now **SQUARE** has its input. This completes both inputs to **AVERAGE**, which completes the entire input to **OUTPUT**.

Generalizing this method, you can see that so long as Logo knows how many inputs each function needs, and so long as each function name is a prefix operator (i.e., it is written to the left of its inputs), then you don't need parentheses at all in writing Logo commands. On the other hand, parentheses help considerably in enabling the human eye to see the pattern. So unless you are very practiced, you should not write a complex expression without parentheses for fear of not being able to read it the next day.

The above rule for parsing expressions is modified for infix operators (i.e., operators that are written between their inputs, rather than to the left of them). In a line such as

WORD 3 + 4   7

---

[6] This rule can be confusing, since the latter expression is more like **SQUARE(X)**, which is what is used in mathematics or in languages like BASIC or Pascal. Keep in mind that parentheses in Logo are used to indicate *grouping*, not as special symbols for delimiting the list of inputs to functions.

the 3 is combined with the 4 by **+** before any unit is assigned as an input to **WORD**, so the line gets broken up as:

WORD (3 + 4) 7

which gives 77. The general rule is that the infix arithmetic operations **+**, **−**, *****, and **/** have higher priority than prefix operators.

Logo's rules for parentheses are designed to enable you to write simple expressions without worrying about parentheses. For complex expressions, it is better to use parentheses to avoid confusion.

Commands with a variable number of inputs

Although we haven't mentioned it yet, certain Logo primitive operations can take a variable number of inputs. One of them is **SENTENCE**, as in the following example:

PRINT (SENTENCE [THE BIG] [BAD] [WOLF])
THE BIG BAD WOLF

which uses one **SENTENCE** operation to combine three things into a list. The fact that **SENTENCE** is combining three things rather than its usual two is indicated by the parentheses grouping **SENTENCE** together with its inputs. In this way, **SENTENCE** can take any number of inputs. Other Logo commands that take a variable number of inputs are **WORD** and **PRINT**. (When **PRINT** is called with more than one input, it prints all its inputs on one line, separated by spaces.)

PRINT (WORD "ONE "TWO "THREE "FOUR)
ONETWOTHREEFOUR

(PRINT "ONE "TWO "THREE "FOUR)
ONE TWO THREE FOUR

The operations **AND** and **OR** also can take variable numbers of inputs:

PRINT (AND (5 = 3) (5 = 4) (5 = 5))
FALSE

PRINT OR (5 = 3) (5 = 4) (5 = 5))
TRUE

Object Logo also permits you to define your own procedures that accept a variable number of inputs, or procedures that accept optional inputs and assign default values to inputs that are not supplied. See the Object Logo Reference Manual for information.

Examples

Here are a few examples illustrating the rules discussed above, including some common errors and their explanations:

PRINT "A "B "C
A
You don't say what to do with B.

The default number of inputs to **PRINT** is 1, so **PRINT** prints its input, which is **A**. Now Logo is faced with the rest of the line, and it runs across the symbol **B**. Since there are no outstanding operations that need inputs, Logo complains that there is nothing to do with the **B**.

(PRINT "A "B "C)
A B C

Here parentheses are correctly used to group the three inputs to **PRINT**.

PRINT ("A "B "C)
Too much inside parentheses.

When you use parentheses to indicate grouping, you should group an operation together with its inputs. The parentheses are being used in this example as they would be used in BASIC, to surround the inputs alone. But Logo always tries to interpret a parenthesized expression as a complete unit, which does not make sense in this case.

CHAPTER **6**

Projects Using Numbers, Words **and Lists**

This chapter presents three open-ended projects using numbers, words and lists, suitable for beginning students. The first project is a simple arithmetic quiz program similar to the drill and practice computer systems used in some schools. The next project shows how to use lists to write programs that generate "random" sentences. We then reprint a paper by Papert and Solomon [23] that describes a simple game-playing program and discusses ideas about how to involve students in planning and carrying out complex projects.

6.1. Arithmetic Quiz Program

Here's a simple arithmetic drill and practice program:

```
QUIZ
HOW MUCH IS 37 + 64
101
GOOD
HOW MUCH IS 29 + 46
87
THE ANSWER IS 75
HOW MUCH IS 21 + 11
32
GOOD
and so on
```

Designing a quiz program that works like this is a good programming project for elementary school students.[1] Here is one of many possible versions:

```
TO QUIZ
MAKE "NUM1 RANDOM 100
MAKE "NUM2 RANDOM 100
MAKE "ANSWER :NUM1 + :NUM2
PRINT (SENTENCE [HOW MUCH IS] :NUM1 [+] :NUM2)
MAKE "REPLY READNUMBER
TEST :REPLY = :ANSWER
IFTRUE [PRINT [GOOD]]
IFFALSE [PRINT SENTENCE [THE ANSWER IS] :ANSWER]
QUIZ
END


TO READNUMBER
OUTPUT FIRST READLIST
END
```

---

[1] And designing such a program is probably a better educational experience than *using* such a program, which is unfortunately much more typical of how computers are currently used in schools.

You use **READNUMBER** rather than **READLIST** directly because **READLIST** outputs a list. If the user types in a single number, **READLIST** outputs a list containing that number as its only item.[2]

You can also modify **READNUMBER** to check that the response is actually a number:

```
TO READNUMBER
MAKE "IN FIRST READLIST
TEST NUMBERP :IN
IFTRUE [OUTPUT :IN]
IFFALSE [PRINT [PLEASE ANSWER WITH A NUMBER]]
IFFALSE [OUTPUT READNUMBER]
END
```

The behavior of **QUIZ** is now:

```
QUIZ
HOW MUCH IS 6 + 14
B0
PLEASE ANSWER WITH A NUMBER
20
GOOD
etc.
```

Observe that the recursive call in the final line of the **READNUMBER** procedure makes the procedure keep asking until the user responds with a number.

QUIZ is a good programming project because it has a simple core, yet there are so many extensions and variations. Some of these are as follows:

- Allowing the user to keep trying a question until getting the correct **answer**
- Keeping score
- Progressing to harder and harder problems when the score is good
- Giving advice

6.2. Random-Sentence Generators

You can have lots of fun with programs that print random sentences. In designing such programs it is very useful to have as a building block a procedure **PICKRANDOM** that takes a list as input and outputs an item selected at random from a list, for example:

```
PRINT PICKRANDOM [EENEY MEENEY MINEY MO]
MEENEY
```

---

[2] Thus, if you set **ANSWER** to be the list returned by **READLIST**, **ANSWER** would never be equal to the sum of **NUM1** and **NUM2** , which is a number. For example, if the user types 7 followed by RETURN, the value returned by **READLIST** will be the list [7], not the number 7. To obtain the number itself, you extract the first item from the list returned by **READLIST**.

```
PRINT PICKRANDOM [EENEY MEENEY MINEY MO]
MO
```

PICKRANDOM is implemented in terms of Logo primitives **ITEM**, which outputs the nth item in a given list, and **COUNT**, which outputs the number of items in a list.

```
TO PICKRANDOM :X
OUTPUT ITEM (1 + RANDOM (COUNT :X)) :X
END
```

Observe how the inputs to **ITEM** and **RANDOM** are chosen. If the **COUNT** of the list **X** is n, then

```
RANDOM (COUNT :X)
```

returns a number selected at random between 0 and $n-1$. You should add 1 to this produce to a random number between 1 and n, which becomes the input to **ITEM**. For beginning users, you can supply the entire **PICKRANDOM** procedure as a "black box."

Once you have **PICKRANDOM**, it is easy to generate simple random sentences of the form {noun} {verb} by picking words at random from lists of nouns and verbs:

```
TO CHATTER
MAKE "NOUNS [DOGS CATS CHILDREN TIGERS]
MAKE "VERBS [RUN BITE TALK LAUGH]
BABBLE
END
```

```
TO BABBLE
PRINT SENTENCE (PICKRANDOM :NOUNS)
              (PICKRANDOM :VERBS)
_
BABBLE
END
```

```
CHATTER
CATS LAUGH
TIGERS TALK
CHILDREN BITE
TIGERS BITE
DOGS TALK
.


.
```

You can make the sentence generator more interesting, by telling the computer occasionally to ask for a new noun or verb to be typed in, and to add it to the corresponding list. For nouns this can be done with

```
TO LEARN.NOUN
PRINT [TEACH ME A NEW NOUN]
MAKE "NOUNS SENTENCE :NOUNS READLIST
END
```

Observe that this uses the **SENTENCE** operation to combine the typed in word with the list of current nouns. You can define a similar **LEARN.VERB** procedure for verbs.

Now you can modify **BABBLE** to ask for a new noun or verb every so often (1 chance in 10):

```
TO BABBLE
IF (RANDOM 10) = 0 [LEARN.NOUN]
IF (RANDOM 10) = 0 [LEARN.VERB]
PRINT SENTENCE (PICKRANDOM :NOUNS)
                (PICKRANDOM :VERBS)
BABBLE
END
```

The behavior of the program is now

```
CHATTER
CHILDREN TALK
TIGERS RUN
TEACH ME A NEW VERB
WALK
DOGS RUN
CATS BITE
TEACH ME A NEW NOUN
BANANAS
DOGS WALK
BANANAS BITE
    .


    .
```

There are many extensions to this project. You can make more complex sentences by adding other parts of speech such as adjectives and adverbs. You can match singular verbs with singular nouns and plural with plural. You can generate random "poetry." Papert [21] describes the experience of one 13-year-old while engaged in such a project:

> One day Jenny came in very excited. She had made a discovery. "Now I know why we have nouns and verbs," she said. For many years in school Jenny had been drilled in grammatical categories. She had never understood the differences between nouns and verbs and adverbs. But now it was apparent that her difficulty with grammar was not due to an inability to work with logical categories. It was something else. She had not been able to make any sense of what grammar was about in the sense of what it might be *for*... But now, as she tried to get the computer to generate poetry, something remarkable happened. She found herself

classifying words into categories, not because she had been told she had to but because she needed to. In order to "teach" her computer to make strings of words that would look like English, she had to "teach" it to choose words of an appropriate class. What she learned about grammar from this experience with a machine was anything but mechanical or routine. Her learning was deep and meaningful. Jenny did more than learn definitions for particular grammatical classes. She understood the general idea that words (like things) can be placed in different groups or sets, and that doing so could work for her. She not only "understood" grammar, she changed her relationship to it.

6.3. Nim: A Game-Playing Program

This section is a slightly modified version of a paper written by Seymour Papert and Cynthia Solomon, which was originally published as an MIT Artificial Intelligence Laboratory Memo [23]. It illustrates some ideas about how to initiate beginning students into the art of planning and writing a program complex enough to be considered a project rather than an exercise on using the language or simple programming ideas.

The project is to write a program to play a simple game ("one-pile Nim" or "21") as invincibly as possible. The project was developed by Papert and Solomon for a class of seventh-grade students taught during 1968-69 at the Muzzey Junior High School in Lexington, Mass. This was the longest programming project these students had encountered, and the intention was to give them a model of how to go about working under these conditions. To achieve this, the teachers worked very hard to develop a clear organization of sub-goals, which they explained to the class at the beginning of the three-week period devoted to this particular program. You would not expect beginners to find as clear a sub-goal structure as this one; but once they have seen a good example, they are more likely find clear sub-goals in the future for other problems. Thus the primary teaching purpose was to develop the idea of splitting a task into sub-goals. The intent was to provide the students with good models of various ways in which this can be done, and to have them experience the heuristic power of this kind of planning (as opposed to jumping straight into writing programs).

A sub-goal structure can be imposed on a problem in several ways. One way is by "chopping," that is, by recognizing that the final program has distinct functions that can be performed by separate subprocedures. But this is not the only way. Many heuristic programs can be simplified rather than chopped. We illustrate this by first writing a procedure to play the entire game of Nim, but in a "dumb way." Once we have done so, we can study its performance, decide why it plays badly and strengthen its play. Thus the successive partial solutions to the problem appear as making a procedure progressively "smarter."

Describing the evolution of the program in this way has the additional benefit of allowing one to make an analogy valuable in two senses: by using themselves as models, students acquire a fertile source of ideas about programming; on the other hand, the experience of debugging programs can have a therapeutic effect in leading them to see their own mistakes as emotionally neutral *bugs* rather than as emotionally charged *errors*.

6.3.1. The Sub-goal Plan

The key idea for subdivision of the problem is to write a series of programs, each of which is "smarter" than the previous one. The first program knows nothing about the strategy of play. It does not generate moves, but asks each of two human players in turn what move to make. For example, it may act as a scorekeeper, just keeping track of the number of sticks without bothering about whether the move is legal. From scorekeeper the machine can advance to referee. This means that it checks the move for legality and eventually declares the game over and announces the winner. After we have a working mechanical referee, we start making a mechanical player. The first version of a player chooses legal, but not necessarily good moves. Indeed, it generates a move randomly, uses its ability as a referee to decide if it is legal, and then either accepts it or generates another random move.

When this works, the child may make the program smarter and smarter by adding features or by writing a completely new version until finally—if all goes well—an infallible strategic player is evolved.

A natural form for programs of intermediate smartness is the following: the program has a list of simple situations in which it knows how to play; in other situations it plays randomly. In other words, it plays by the form of strategy used by most children in most strategic games.

In working with a class, a good moment should be seized to prod the students into noting and discussing the analogy between this very simple heuristic program and themselves—particularly, how the program gets to be smarter through more or better knowledge. Seeing the program as a cognitive model is a valuable and exciting experience for the students. They can easily be drawn into discussion about how meaningful such models are. To keep the discussion alive, the teacher should be equipped with arguments and examples to counteract extremist, and so sterile, positions. For example, if the students feel that the program is too simple to be a model of human thinking, the teacher might discuss whether a toy airplane is a useful model of a jet-airplane. Does it work by the same principles? Can you learn about airliners by studying toy models? On the other hand, if a class swings over to the position that there really is no difference, the teacher can ask questions about whether the program could learn by itself without a programmer. If this is too enthusiastically accepted it is well for the teacher to ask: "How much do you learn without being told?" Ideally, the teacher should merely guide the discussion without having to say any of this. But awareness of such argument will permit more sensitive guiding. An interesting exercise and base for discussion is to have the students study various programs of intermediate smartness, classify their bad moves by degrees of stupidity, and give the program grades (or say why they think doing so is silly!).

The stratification of the project has the good feature of allowing students to find their own levels. A slower child who gets only as far as the random player, nevertheless has the taste of success if his program does what it does well. Tendencies to feel inferior should be counteracted by the teacher's attitude and by the teacher's encouraging individual variations so that no child's final program is a mere subset of a more advanced one. The teacher's computer culture can be very relevant in this delicate kind of situation. Although the richness of programming permits students to generate many fertile ideas, sensitive filtering by the teacher can enormously improve the achievement-to-frustration ratio.

First steps with the students

A move in Nim consists of taking one, two, or three matchsticks from a given pile. Two players move alternately. The player who takes the last stick wins.

The first step is to see that everyone knows the rules and understands what the first program does, for example, by imitating its function or by writing imaginary scripts. In the course of discussing this the teacher introduces some names so the class can talk about what the program is doing.

Here is an example of a script:

```
THE NUMBER OF STICKS IS 8
JOAN TO PLAY.  WHAT'S YOUR MOVE?
2
THE NUMBER OF STICKS IS 6
BILL TO PLAY.  WHAT'S YOUR MOVE?
3
THE NUMBER OF STICKS IS 3
JOAN TO PLAY.  WHAT'S YOUR MOVE?
3
JOAN IS THE WINNER!
```

Later in the project the teacher can insist that students consider what happens when a player replies to **WHAT'S YOUR MOVE** by **5** or **COW**. In the beginning the teacher should discourage all but the most competent students from worrying about "funny" answers before getting the program to work with normal answers.

Examining the script you see that there must be names for:

- The current number of sticks—say **STICKS**
- The move—say **MOVE**
- The next player—say **PLAYER**
- And, a little more subtle, the other player—say **OPPONENT**

To be sure that everyone understands, they are asked to fill in these "Logo things" for successive rounds, following the previous script.

Round No.	:STICKS	:PLAYER	:OPPONENT	:MOVE
1	8	JOAN	BILL	2
2	?	?	JOAN	3
3	3	?	?	?

6.3.2. A Simple Scorekeeper

If this is the first game-playing program, the teacher builds up to it by asking some standard questions:

- What shall we call the procedure? (Let's say **NIMPLAY**)
- What must **NIMPLAY** do?
- What must **NIMPLAY** know?

Possible answers are

- Announce the remaining number of sticks.
- Announce the player to move.
- Get the move and make all the modifications.
- Recurse.

To do this, **NIMPLAY** must remember **:STICKS**, **:PLAYER**, and **:OPPONENT** from the previous round and get **:MOVE** by asking for it. The first three things must passed from one call to **NIMPLAY** to the next so they should be inputs. On the other hand, **:MOVE** comes from the human player, so it does not need to be an input. If you look ahead, you may notice that later on, **:MOVE** will sometimes come from a procedure—that is, when the machine gets to be smart enough to make its own moves. So to keep the door open for changes, the problems of getting **:MOVE** and using it are separated. The standard way to do this is to plan on a subprocedure—say, called **GETMOVE**.

Now students can write **NIMPLAY**:

```
TO NIMPLAY :STICKS :PLAYER :OPPONENT
        ;When in doubt, have lots of inputs.
PRINT SENTENCE [THE NUMBER OF STICKS IS] :STICKS
        ;Announce the number of sticks.
PRINT SENTENCE :PLAYER [TO PLAY.  WHAT'S YOUR MOVE?]
MAKE "NEWSTICKS :STICKS - GETMOVE
        ;Pretend GETMOVE has already been written.
NIMPLAY :NEWSTICKS :OPPONENT :PLAYER
        ;Recursion line.  Notice how :PLAYER
        ;and :OPPONENT are reversed
END
```

```
TO GETMOVE
MAKE "MOVE READNUMBER
          ;See READNUMBER procedure in section 6.1.
OUTPUT :MOVE
END
```

From scorekeeper to referee

As referee the program has some new tasks:

- To decide whether the game is over
- To declare the winner if it is over
- To make sure that :PLAYER takes 1, 2, or 3 sticks each time

The first two tasks are achieved by adding a test and a stop line to NIMPLAY. For example,

```
TEST :NEWSTICKS = 0
IFTRUE [PRINT SENTENCE :PLAYER  [IS THE WINNER!]]
IFTRUE [STOP]
```

The third task can be accomplished by giving GETMOVE a "try-again" form, using the MEMBERP predicate which takes an item and a lists as inputs and checks whether the item is in the list.

```
TO GETMOVE
PRINT [YOU MAY TAKE 1, 2, or 3 STICKS]
MAKE "MOVE READNUMBER
TEST MEMBERP :MOVE [1 2 3]
IFFALSE [OUTPUT GETMOVE]
          ;If the test is false, try again.
OUTPUT :MOVE
END
```

With these changes, NIMPLAY is certainly a referee—but still has some rough edges. For example, when :STICKS is 2, GETMOVE gives permission to take 1, 2, or 3 sticks! And if :PLAYER takes 3 sticks, :STICKS becomes negative, and the game will go on forever, because of a "slip-by" bug. However, we shall leave it as an exercise to remedy these minor failings.

In presenting this section to students, the teacher may want to work through one of the two major modifications with the class and let the students struggle with the other. The slip-by bug we would leave to the class to discover and cure. Those who miss it at this stage will find its presence more obtrusive later. If so, a profitable discussion may develop on the question of why the bug was not found—perhaps because the human player always makes reasonable moves so that :STICKS never becomes negative even though the machine allows it. Later we shall see that when the machine makes its own moves, it is not so cooperative unless it is told to be.

Examples of individual frills to a referee program are: timing moves, declaring the winner a move or two ahead (!), allowing a player to take a move back, printing a score sheet, giving advice (!), establishing and imposing handicaps (!), and changing the rules.

6.3.3. A Mechanical Player

How can the machine choose a move? The simplest way is by using **PICKRANDOM**.[3] For example, you could allow **GETMOVE** to make the choice:[4] if a person is to play, use **READNUMBER**; if the machine is to play, use **PICKRANDOM**. But it has to be told whether the player is human or the computer. So it must have an input.

```
TO GETMOVE :PLAYER
TEST :PLAYER = [COMPUTER]
IFTRUE [MAKE "MOVE PICKRANDOM [1 2 3]]
IFFALSE [PRINT [YOU MAY TAKE 1, 2, OR 3 STICKS]]
IFFALSE [MAKE "MOVE READNUMBER]
   .

   .
```

as before.

At this stage the slip-by bug may become serious. One way to kill it is to tell **GETMOVE** about **:STICKS** and have it try again if **:MOVE** comes up greater than **:STICKS** . To do this you change the title line to:

```
TO GETMOVE  :PLAYER :STICKS
```

and add a pair of lines after the two **MAKE**s.

```
TEST :MOVE > :STICKS
IFTRUE [OUTPUT GETMOVE :PLAYER :STICKS]
```

Strategic play

The plan for writing the Nim playing program in many strata now calls for it to recognize a few special numbers and know what to do in those cases, but continue to play stupidly in other cases. However, by this time it is likely that the class has already discovered the full strategy. It may still be worthwhile to encourage at least some member to follow the original plan as an instructive joke. In this section we illustrate a general question-answer technique for classroom discussion to encourage habits of heuristic neatness in the students' own thinking.

A good exercise is to observe **NIMPLAY** in its present condition,

---

[3] The **PICKRANDOM** procedure (section 6.2) can be written by the teacher and given to students as a "primitive."

[4] Notice this anthropomorphism. We find it useful to talk of procedures as agents, of their "state of knowledge," of "telling them," of having them "talk to" one another. And we present this to students as a deliberate metaphor that they may find useful.

and to collect and classify its mistakes. An example of a classification made by a student is:

- **DUMB MISTAKES**
    - * There were five sticks and the machine took two. (If the machine had any sense, it would leave the opponent with four.)
    - * There were six or seven sticks and the machine did not leave four.

- **SUPER DUMB MISTAKES**
    - * There were two or three sticks and the machine did not take all!

We shall write a procedure to avoid first "super dumb mistakes" and then "dumb mistakes".

- Question: What program form? Answer: **TEST.**
- Question: What do we test for? English answer: Whether there are one, two, or three sticks. Logo answer: **TEST MEMBER? :STICKS [1 2 3]**.
- Question: What is the action if the test is passed? English answer: Take all the sticks. Logo answer: **OUTPUT :STICKS**.
- Question: What if it is not passed? English answer: Move just like before. Logo answer: **MAKE "MOVE PICKRANDOM [1 2 3]**.

Now put this together to make a procedure to make the move:

- Question: What must the procedure know? Answer: **:STICKS**—so it needs an input.

```
TO MAKEMOVE :STICKS
TEST MEMBERP :STICKS [1 2 3]
IFTRUE [OUTPUT :STICKS]
IFFALSE [OUTPUT PICKRANDOM [1 2 3]]
END
```

The procedure is used in place of **PICKRANDOM** in **GETMOVE**. So don't forget to change **GETMOVE**!

Now extra lines can be added. For example:

```
TEST :STICKS = 5
IFTRUE [OUTPUT 1]
```

The smart player

By this time everyone should be very close to understanding the strategy, for example, in the following form:

- Question: How does the game end? Answer: When a player *leaves zero* sticks.

So let's try making the main actor be the number of sticks we leave. If we can leave zero that's great. But if we have more than three we can't. So we must think ahead.

- Question: What can we leave to help us leave zero next time? Answer: Four. Because the opponent will leave one, two, or three.
- Question: What can we leave so as to be able to leave four next time? Answer: Eight.
- Question: So 0, 4, 8 are good numbers to shoot at for leaving. What others? Answer: 12, 16, ...
- Question: How could you describe the numbers 0, 4, 8, 12, 16, ... Answer: They are all divisible by 4. **REMAINDER :NUMBER 4 is** 0.
- \$64 Question: If I give you **:NUMBER** , how can you use it to find the next number down divisible by 4? Answer: Subtract **REMAINDER :NUMBER 4.**

So there we are! The smart invincible Nim player is made by replacing **MAKEMOVE** by **SMARTMOVE**:

```
TO SMARTMOVE :STICKS
MAKE "REM REMAINDER :STICKS 4
IF :REM = 0 [OUTPUT 1]
        ;It really doesn't matter in this case.
OUTPUT :REM
END
```

6.3.4. Frills and Modifications

Write superprocedures or make additions to the present procedure to produce transcripts such as the one following.

```
NIM
DO YOU KNOW HOW TO PLAY NIM?
NO
HERE ARE THE RULES:  YOU WILL BE SHOWN A COLLECTION
OF X'S.
YOU MAY REMOVE 1, 2, or 3.  THE PLAYER WHO TAKES THE
LAST X
WINS.  THIS IS PROBABLY TOO VAGUE FOR YOU TO UNDER-
STAND,
BUT TRY PLAYING AND I'LL CORRECT YOUR MISTAKES.

ARE YOU READY?
I AM
PLEASE SAY "YES" OR "NO"
YES
OK.  NOW TELL ME THE NAME OF THE FIRST PLAYER.
JOAN
```

```
NOW THE NAME OF THE OTHER PLAYER
COMPUTER
HOW MANY STICKS DO YOU WANT TO START WITH?
THIRTY-ONE
I'M A DUMB COMPUTER.  TYPE A PROPER NUMERAL.
31
JOAN TO PLAY.
THERE ARE 31 STICKS.
XXXXXXXXXXXXXXXXXXXXXXXXXXXXXXX
JOAN, TAKE 1, 2, OR 3
3

COMPUTER TO PLAY.
THERE ARE 28 STICKS.
XXXXXXXXXXXXXXXXXXXXXXXXXXXX
I TAKE 1

JOAN TO PLAY.
THERE ARE 27 STICKS.
XXXXXXXXXXXXXXXXXXXXXXXXXXX
TAKE 1, 2, OR 3
3

.
```

In addition to such frills, there are unlimited possibilities to play with the ideas in the procedure after it has been made to work. Here are three examples to illustrate the idea that the project has not necessarily run out when the procedure is debugged:

- An interesting simple modification to the rule of the game is to change the 1-2-3 rule to a 1-2 rule or a 1-2-3-4-5 rule. Write a procedure that asks what rule is to be used, and then plays by that rule.
- Our stop rule was: the player who takes the last stick wins. Change this to: whoever takes the last stick loses. (The latter is the traditional form.)
- The game can be embedded in a more complex one, such as moving counters along marked paths on a board. If there is just one linear path, the problem is identical, but if branches are allowed, interesting complexities arise.

6.3.5. A Listing of the NIMPLAY Procedures

Here is a listing of the final form of the **NIMPLAY** procedures. Besides the three procedures listed below, the project also makes use of the **READNUMBER** procedure of section 6.1.

```
TO NIMPLAY :STICKS :PLAYER :OPPONENT
PRINT SENTENCE [THE NUMBER OF STICKS IS] :STICKS
PRINT SENTENCE :PLAYER
                      [TO PLAY.  WHAT'S YOUR MOVE?]
MAKE "NEWSTICKS
_     :STICKS – (GETMOVE :PLAYER :STICKS)
TEST :NEWSTICKS = 0
IFTRUE [PRINT SENTENCE :PLAYER [IS THE WINNER!]]
IFTRUE [STOP]
NIMPLAY :NEWSTICKS :OPPONENT :PLAYER
END


TO GETMOVE :PLAYER :STICKS
TEST :PLAYER = [COMPUTER]
IFTRUE [MAKE "MOVE SMARTMOVE :STICKS]
IFFALSE [PRINT [YOU MAY TAKE 1, 2, OR 3  STICKS]]
IFFALSE [MAKE  "MOVE READNUMBER]
TEST MEMBERP :MOVE [1 2 3]
IFFALSE [OUTPUT GETMOVE :PLAYER :STICKS]
TEST :MOVE > :STICKS
IFTRUE [OUTPUT GETMOVE :PLAYER :STICKS ]
OUTPUT :MOVE
END

TO SMARTMOVE :STICKS
MAKE "REM REMAINDER :STICKS 4
IF :REM = 0 [OUTPUT 1]
OUTPUT :REM
END
```

CHAPTER **7**

Object-Oriented Programming

The most important feature that distinguishes Object Logo from other versions of the Logo language is Object Logo's extensive support for *object-oriented programming*. Object-oriented programming is a way of programming whose roots go back to the computer language Simula, designed during the 1960's by Kristen Nygaard and Ole-Johan Dahl of the Norwegian Computing Center. As the name "Simula" suggests, object-oriented programming is especially powerful for dealing with simulations, where you structure computer programs in terms of "objects" that have specified behavior. The original Logo turtle developed in 1968, whose behavior included the ability to go forward and back and to turn right and left, was an early example of a programming object, although a very restricted one. During the past few years, object-oriented programming has become recognized as an extremely powerful programming methodology, and a number of computer languages organized around object-oriented programming have become popular. These include Smalltalk, C++, the Common Lisp Object System (CLOS) and Object Pascal. However, just as Logo is one of the simplest computer languages to learn, Object Logo is one of the easiest object-oriented systems to use.[1]

The two basic concepts in object-oriented programming are *objects* and *inheritance*. An object is a collection of procedures and data that work together to implement some kind of behavior. An object's procedures (sometimes called the object's *methods*) represent the kinds of things that the object knows how to do. Once you have defined a type of object, you can make multiple copies (also called multiple *instances*) of the object to produce multiple creatures that have the same behavior.

Inheritance is the ability to define new kinds of objects in terms of previously-defined objects. For example, you could define a "frog" to be a kind of turtle that also knows how to hop. When you say that the frog is "a kind of" turtle, you are automatically specifying that the frog knows all the usual turtle methods—forward, back, left, right, and so on. The frog is said to *inherit* these methods from the turtle. It is only the new method (hop) that you have to define explicitly.

Object Logo provides an extensive system to support object-oriented programming, and in this chapter we will only scratch the surface. Since the turtle is such a natural example of a Logo object,

---

[1] Object Logo is based on a unique object system designed at the MIT Artificial Intelligence Laboratory by Gary Drescher.

we will focus mostly on turtle objects and on objects that inherit methods from turtles.

7.1. Multiple Turtles

To show how objects work, we'll start by creating several turtles and make them interact. Normally in Object Logo there is a single "default" turtle, which appears in the Graphics window when you give turtle commands. Instead of using the default turtle, you can create new turtles. For example you can create a turtle named Jareth. You specify that Jareth is to be a **KINDOF** turtle. Then you ask Jareth to **EXIST**:

```
MAKE "JARETH KINDOF TURTLE
ASK :JARETH [EXIST]
```

Asking an object to exist initializes certain information that is associated with the object. Each turtle, for instance, has an associated position and heading, which are initialized when the turtle first exists. At this point, the turtle will appear in the Graphics window. Now you can ask Jareth to go forward:

```
ASK :JARETH [FORWARD 100]
```

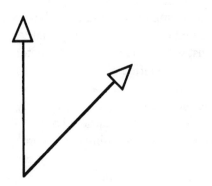

Figure 7.1: Two turtles

As the example shows, you issue a command to an object by using **ASK**. Indicate which object you are asking, and enclose the command in brackets.

You can create a second turtle that moves separately from Jareth. The two turtles are shown in figure 7.1.

```
MAKE "SEBASTIAN KINDOF TURTLE
ASK :SEBASTIAN [EXIST]
ASK :SEBASTIAN [RIGHT 45]
ASK :SEBASTIAN [FORWARD 100]
```

Each turtle has its own position and heading:

```
PRINT ASK :SEBASTIAN [POS]
70.71075439453125     70.71075439453125
```

```
PRINT ASK :JARETH [POS]
0.     100.
```

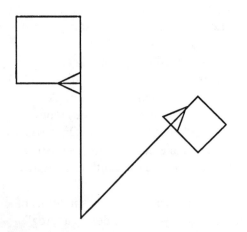

Figure 7.2: Using the **TALKTO** command

7.1.1. ASK and TALKTO

Instead of using **ASK**, another way to issue commands to an individual object is with the command **TALKTO**. Once you specify that you are talking to a particular object, all commands go directly to that object until you specify another object to talk to. Figure 7.2 shows the result of talking to Sebastian and then to Jareth, asking each of them to draw a square as follows:

```
TALKTO :SEBASTIAN
SQUARE 30
TALKTO :JARETH
LEFT 90
SQUARE 50
```

To stop talking to an individual object, and direct commands to Logo in general, you type

TALKTO LOGO

7.1.2. KINDOF and ONEOF

To create a new object, you can use either **KINDOF** or **ONEOF**. The difference between the two commands is that, with **KINDOF**, you must explicitly ask the object to **EXIST** in order to initialize values for the object's variables. **ONEOF** will automatically asks the object to **EXIST**. It's more convenient to use **ONEOF** when you want to make an object to use on its own. It is more convenient to use **KINDOF** when you create an object that you plan to use as a template for creating other objects.

When you create objects with **ONEOF**, you can specify initial values for some of the object's variables. For example

MAKE "ARIES (ONEOF TURTLE "POS [50 100])

makes a turtle whose initial position is (50, 100). Other initial values you can specify include **HEADING, PENCOLOR, PENPATTERN, PENSIZE, PENMODE, SHOWNP, MYWINDOW,** and **DUCKP.**

7.1.3. Turtles Interacting

Here is a simple example using multiple turtles. Start by creating four turtles located at the vertices of a square:

MAKE "JARETH (ONEOF TURTLE "POS [0 0])
MAKE "SEBASTIAN (ONEOF TURTLE "POS [100 0])
MAKE "WALDO (ONEOF TURTLE "POS [0 100])
MAKE "WICKETT (ONEOF TURTLE "POS [100 100])

A turtle will follow another turtle by setting its heading in the direction of the other turtle and moving forward a little bit:

```
TO FOLLOW :WHO
SETHEADING TOWARDS ASK :WHO [POS]
FORWARD 1
END
```

Now make each turtle keep following the turtle to its left:

Figure 7.3: Four turtles start at the vertices of a square—each one follows the turtle to its left

```
TO PATH
ASK :JARETH [FOLLOW :WALDO]
ASK :WALDO [FOLLOW :WICKETT]
ASK :WICKETT [FOLLOW :SEBASTIAN]
ASK :SEBASTIAN [FOLLOW :JARETH]
PATH
END
```

Figures 7.3 and 7.4 show the turtles starting out, and their resulting spiral paths.

7.2. Creating New Types of Objects

Figure 7.4: Complete spiral paths followed by the four turtles

In addition to duplicating an object, you can also make objects that have new behaviors. Start by copying an object, as before. Here, for instance, is a "hopper," which will start out as a kind of turtle:

MAKE "HOPPER KINDOF TURTLE

Since the hopper is a kind of turtle, it inherits all the things a turtle knows how to do—**FORWARD, BACK, LEFT, RIGHT,** and so on. In addition, you can teach the hopper a new procedure: **TO MOVE.** To do this, you type **ASK :HOPPER** followed by the title of the procedure in brackets. Then type the rest of the procedure lines, and finally **END:**

```
ASK :HOPPER  [TO MOVE :DISTANCE]
REPEAT :DISTANCE / 20
_ [RT 45 FD SQRT 200
_ LT 90 BK SQRT 200
_ RT 45 WAIT 1/2]
END
```

Figure 7.5: ASK :HOPPER [EXIST]
          ASK :HOPPER [MOVE 150]

Figure 7.5 shows how a hopper moves.
You can also make another kind of object, called a flyer, which has its own method of moving, as shown in figure 7.6.

MAKE "FLYER KINDOF TURTLE

Figure 7.6: ASK :FLYER [EXIST]
          ASK :FLYER [MOVE 150]

```
ASK :FLYER [TO MOVE :DISTANCE]
WAIT 1/4
RT 45
FD SQRT 800
RT 45
WAIT 1/3
FD :DISTANCE - 40
WAIT 1/3
LT 135
BK SQRT 800
WAIT 1/4
RT 45
END
```

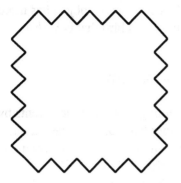

Figure 7.7: ASK :HOPPER [SQUAREMOVE 100]

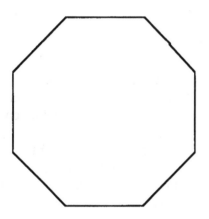

Figure 7.8: ASK :FLYER [SQUAREMOVE 100]

7.3. Inheritance

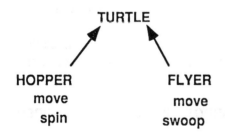

Figure 7.9: The inheritance hierarchy relating hopper, flyer, and turtle

Hopper and flyer are both kinds of turtles, but each one has its own way to move. For example, suppose you define the procedure

```
TO SQUAREMOVE :DISTANCE
REPEAT 4 [MOVE :DISTANCE RIGHT 90]
END
```

If you ask the hopper and flyer to **SQUAREMOVE** they will draw different designs, as shown in figures 7.7 and 7.8. This is because the hopper and the flyer each use their own **MOVE** as part of **SQUAREMOVE**.

You can teach your objects as many procedures as you want. For example, you can teach a hopper to **SPIN**, and a flyer to **SWOOP**:

```
ASK :HOPPER [TO SPIN]
REPEAT 3 * 360 [RT 1]
END
```

```
ASK :FLYER [TO SWOOP :DISTANCE]
FD 100
RT 90
REPEAT :DISTANCE / 20 [ FD 20 ARCRIGHT 20 360]
WAIT 1/4
LT 90
BK 100
END
```

Because **SPIN** is defined only for a hopper, a flyer does not know how to **SPIN**.

```
ASK :FLYER [SPIN]
You haven't told me how to SPIN.
```
Likewise a hopper does not know how to **SWOOP**.

```
ASK :HOPPER [SWOOP 150]
You haven't told me how to SWOOP.
```

Figure 7.9 shows the *inheritance hierarchy* relating hopper, flyer and turtle. Turtle is said to be the *parent* of hopper and flyer. Whenever you ask an object to do something, the object first looks to see if it has a command of that name, then if its parent has a command of that name, then its parent's parent, and so on. A flyer knows how to **SWOOP** because **SWOOP** was defined for **FLYER**. A flyer knows how to **FORWARD** because its parent, **TURTLE**, knows how to **FORWARD**.

7.3.1. Multiple Inheritance

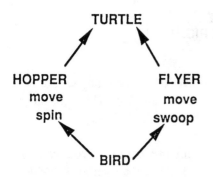

Figure 7.10: The inheritance hierarchy for bird

7.3.2. Method Override

The inheritance rules can be complicated when an object has more than one parent. For instance, you can make a bird that is *both* a kind of hopper and a kind of flyer.

MAKE "BIRD KINDOF (LIST :HOPPER :FLYER)

As the example shows, you make something with multiple parents by giving **KINDOF** a list of the parents, rather than just a single parent. Figure 7.10 shows the inheritance hierarchy for bird. As you can see from the diagram, a bird can go **FORWARD, BACK, LEFT,** and **RIGHT** (which it inherits from turtle); a bird can **SPIN** (which it inherits from hopper); and a bird can **SWOOP** (which it inherits from flyer).

How will a bird **MOVE**? Will it move like a flyer or like a hopper? The answer is that a bird will move like a hopper, because hopper was the first parent named in the list. If instead, the definition had been

MAKE "BIRD KINDOF (LIST :FLYER :HOPPER)

then a bird would move like a flyer.

You can give an object a method that has the same name as a method that one of its parents has. As you would expect, the object will use its own method definition, rather than the method definition of the parent. This is called *method overriding*.

If you need to explicitly refer to the parent's method, rather than to the object's own method, you use the prefix **USUAL**. For example, you can make a new object that is a kind of turtle, and teach it to go **FORWARD** differently than a regular turtle:

MAKE "CREEPER KINDOF TURTLE

ASK :CREEPER [TO FORWARD :DISTANCE]
REPEAT :DISTANCE [USUAL.FORWARD 1]
END

A creeper goes **FORWARD** very slowly by taking repeated steps of (turtle) **FORWARD 1**. In the definition of the creeper's **FORWARD** there is a reference to the turtle's **FORWARD** as **USUAL.FORWARD**.

These methods with the same name are inherited just like other methods. For instance, suppose you make something that is both a hopper and a creeper:

MAKE "CREEPYHOPPER KINDOF (LIST :CREEPER :HOPPER)

If you ask a creepyhopper to move, it will follow the same pattern as a hopper, only at the speed of a creeper. The creepyhopper inherits the **MOVE** method from the hopper. The **MOVE** procedure, however, uses **FORWARD**. The creepyhopper uses the creeper's **FORWARD** method rather than the ordinary **FORWARD** used by hopper.[2]

7.3.3. Changing a Turtle's Shape

As an example of inheritance and method override, you can make turtle objects that have their own special shapes, and combine these with other kinds of turtles. To define a turtle with a special shape, you define for it procedures called **DRAWTURTLE** and **ERASETURTLE**. Object Logo will call these procedures automatically whenever a turtle moves, to draw the turtle's shape at its new position and to erase the shape at the old position. Here is the definition of a **SHAPETURTLE** object:

```
MAKE "SHAPETURTLE KINDOF TURTLE

ASK :SHAPETURTLE [TO DRAWTURTLE]
MAKE "SAVE PENMODE
SETPENMODE "REVERSE
DRAWSHAPE
SETPENMODE :SAVE
END

ASK :SHAPETURTLE [TO ERASETURTLE]
MAKE "SAVE PENMODE
SETPENMODE "REVERSE
DRAWSHAPE
SETPENMODE :SAVE
END
```

The **SHAPETURTLE** expects to have a procedure called **DRAWSHAPE** that actually draws the required shape. **DRAWTURTLE** and **ERASETURTLE** both call the same **DRAWSHAPE** procedure with the pen mode set to reverse. way, the shape will appear at the new position, where visible, and it will be erased at the old position. **DRAWTURTLE** and **ERASETURTLE** save the old pen mode, set the pen mode to reverse, call **DRAWSHAPE**, and restore the pen mode.

You can combine a hopper and a shapeturtle to make a turtle that can hop, but which also has its own special shape:

```
MAKE "JAXOM KINDOF (LIST :SHAPETURTLE :HOPPER)

ASK :JAXOM [TO DRAWSHAPE]
MAKE "START POS
RIGHT 35
```

---

[2] A hoppycreeper, defined by
MAKE "HOPPYCREEPER KINDOF (LIST :HOPPER :CREEPER)
would also go **FORWARD** like a creeper, even though **:HOPPER** is listed first. This is because the **HOPPER** does not have an explicit **FORWARD** method of its own. When looking for the correct **FORWARD** method to apply, Object Logo tries **HOPPER** and then **CREEPER** before going all the way back to turtle. See the Object Logo Reference Manual for a complete description of the inheritance rules.

Figure 7.11: Shape of the Jaxom turtle

```
FORWARD 50
RIGHT 125
FORWARD 15
RIGHT 145
FORWARD 7
LEFT 180
RIGHT 55
FORWARD 30
RIGHT 90
SETPOS :START
RIGHT 90
END
```

Figure 7.12: ASK :JAXOM [EXIST]
ASK :JAXOM [MOVE 100]

Jaxom appears as in figure 7.11. Because Jaxom is a turtle, it can go **FORWARD**, **LEFT**, **RIGHT**, and **BACK**, but it can also **MOVE**, as in figure 7.12, because it is a hopper.

7.4. Objects Not Based On Turtles

All the objects presented so far in this chapter have been kinds of turtles. By using inheritance, you can begin with a turtle object and then modify its built-in behavior to create your own specialized graphical objects. In a similar way, Object Logo provides many other built-in types of objects, including windows, files, menus, MIDI and robotics, that make it easy to do advanced programming projects on the Macintosh. You can find details on these objects and how to use them in the Object Logo Reference Manual.

You can also create objects from scratch that don't have any procedures defined for them, except for the ones you define explicitly. The Logo primitive **SOMETHING** returns a new "blank" object that you can give whatever behavior you like. For example, you can make a cat and a dog and teach each one to speak in its own way:

```
MAKE "DOG SOMETHING

ASK :DOG [TO SPEAK]
PRINT [WUF WUF!]
END

MAKE "CAT SOMETHING

ASK :CAT [TO SPEAK]
PRINT [MEOW MEOW PURRR!]
END

ASK :DOG [SPEAK]
WUF WUF!

ASK :CAT [SPEAK]
MEOW MEOW PURRR!
```

All the concepts described in this chapter—inheritance, multiple inheritance and method override—apply to these kinds of objects, just as they do to turtles. Here, for example, is a mean dog, defined as a kind of dog that overrides the normal **SPEAK** procedure:

```
MAKE "MEANDOG KINDOF :DOG

ASK :MEANDOG [TO SPEAK]
USUAL.SPEAK
PRINT [GGGRRRRRRR!]
END

ASK :MEANDOG [SPEAK]
WUF WUF!
GGGRRRRRRR!
```

CHAPTER **8**

Writing Interactive Programs

We've already seen examples of Logo programs that use **PRINT** to print information on the display screen, and programs that use **READLIST** to input information from the keyboard. This chapter reviews these commands and describes more elaborate ways of handling input and output. As an example, we show how to create "instant response" Logo systems for very young children. We also show how a Logo-based "dynaturtle" can be used to introduce elementary school children to computer projects involving motion and simple physics.

8.1. Controlling Screen Output

The Logo **PRINT** command, as used throughout the preceding chapters, is the main command for showing information on the display screen. **PRINT** takes a word or a list as an input, types it on the screen, and moves the cursor to the next line. (Remember that lists are printed without the outer brackets.) Although we have so far used **PRINT** with only one input, it can also take a variable number of inputs, providing that the word **PRINT** and the inputs are enclosed in parentheses, as explained in section 5.7.2. When **PRINT** is used with more than one input, it prints all the inputs on the same line, separated by spaces. For example:

```
MAKE "COLOR "GREEN
MAKE "TASTE "SOUR
(PRINT [THIS APPLE IS] :COLOR "AND :TASTE)
THIS APPLE IS GREEN AND SOUR
```

The command **TYPE** is just like **PRINT**, except that it does not move the cursor to a new line after printing. Compare

```
TO COUNTUP :X
PRINT :X
COUNTUP :X + 1
END

COUNTUP 1
1
2
3
```

```
TO COUNTUP1 :X
TYPE :X
TYPE ",
COUNTUP1 :X + 1
END

COUNTUP1 1
1,2,3,...
```

The **CLEARTEXT** command clears the Listener Window.

8.2. Keyboard Input

The **READLIST** operation is used to read input from the keyboard, as shown in section 5.4. **READLIST** causes the computer to wait for you to type in a line (terminated by RETURN) and then outputs that line as a list. Remember that what you type in will *always be interpreted as a list*. For example, if you type in a single word, **READLIST** returns a list containing that word:

```
MAKE "ANS READLIST
100
IF :ANS = 100  [PRINT  "YES]
<nothing is printed>
IF :ANS = [100]  [PRINT  "YES]
YES
```

In addition to the "line at a time" input from **READLIST,** Logo also provides "character at a time" input through the command **READCHAR** (abbreviated **RC**). **READCHAR** causes the computer to pause and wait for you to type in a single character (without RETURN) and then outputs the character that was typed:

```
MAKE "ANS READCHAR
X
IF :ANS =  "X  [PRINT  "YES]
YES
```

8.2.1. Example: Instant Response for Very Young Children

The following program uses **READCHAR** to provide "instant response" control of the turtle for drawing:

```
TO INSTANT
COMMAND
INSTANT
END

TO COMMAND
MAKE "COM READCHAR
IF :COM = "F [FORWARD 10]
IF :COM = "R [RIGHT 30]
IF :COM = "L [LEFT 30]
IF :COM = "C [CLEARSCREEN]
END
```

This program causes the turtle to move in response to individual keystrokes: **F** for forward, **L** for left, **R** for right, and **C** for clearing the screen and starting over. It can form a good tool for using computer graphics with very young children. This same instant-response mechanism is also useful in designing languages for use by the physically handicapped, for which it is important to minimize the number of keystrokes required.

It is easy to increase the repertoire of this **INSTANT** language by adding additional lines to the **COMMAND** procedure. For example, if you want the **S** key to make the turtle draw a small square, you define a procedure called **SQUARE** (say, that draws a square of side 20) and add to **COMMAND** the line

```
IF :COM = "S [SQUARE]
```

Section 10.2.1 discusses more elaborate extensions to **INSTANT**.

8.2.2. Keyboard Control of an Ongoing Process

Notice that **READLIST** and **READCHAR** both make the computer *stop and wait* for something to be typed. Logo also allows you to write programs in which the keyboard is used to control an ongoing process. That is, if a character is typed at the keyboard, the program is able to respond to the character; but if nothing is typed, the program is able to keep running anyway. Such programs are implemented in Logo using the **KEYP** command. **KEYP** outputs **TRUE** or **FALSE** depending on whether a character has been typed at the keyboard. When **KEYP** is **TRUE**, the next **READCHAR** command returns the character that was typed, otherwise **READCHAR** has to wait until a character is typed.[1]

For example, you can modify the **INSTANT** program so that it makes the turtle move forward *continually*, turning right or left in response to the letters **R** and **L** typed at the keyboard. We'll call the resulting program **DRIVE**:

```
TO DRIVE
FORWARD 1
COMMAND
DRIVE
END
```

---

[1] More specifically, characters typed at the keyboard are saved in an input buffer. **READCHAR** reads characters from the buffer one by one. **KEYP** outputs **TRUE** if the buffer is not empty. If Logo is doing a lot of processing in between characters, and if one types characters very fast, a sequence of characters may build up in the buffer, and the program may seem to "fall behind" in its responses to the typed characters. For some applications, it may be acceptable to fix this problem by simply ignoring the unprocessed characters. This can be done by periodically using the **CLEARINPUT** command, which clears any characters from the input buffer.

```
TO COMMAND
MAKE "COM READKEY
IF :COM = "R [RIGHT 30]
IF :COM = "L [LEFT 30]
IF :COM = "C [CLEARSCREEN]
END
```

The difference between this program and **INSTANT** is that the turtle goes forward each time, rather than when an **F** is typed. Whereas the **COMMAND** program used by **INSTANT** calls **READCHAR**, the **COMMAND** program used in **DRIVE** calls **READKEY**. **READKEY** is a procedure that, if a character has been typed, outputs that character, and otherwise outputs the empty word. **READKEY** is implemented using **KEYP**:

```
TO READKEY
IF KEYP [OUTPUT READCHAR]
OUTPUT "
END
```

READKEY is a good example of a useful "primitive" that can be supplied by the teacher to students working on interactive programming projects.

8.3. Example: The Dynaturtle Program

DYNATURTLE is an extension of the Logo turtle, developed by Andy diSessa as a computer-based physics environment for elementary school students. It has also been used as an experimental setting for investigating the role of intuition in learning physics. See A. diSessa [9] for details. This section, based on a paper by Dan Watt, is a description of **DYNATURTLE** that can be used by students and teachers.

8.3.1. What is a Dynamic Turtle?

A *dynamic* turtle or *dynaturtle* behaves as though it were a rocket ship in outer space. To make it move you have to give it a *kick* by "firing a rocket." It then *keeps moving* in the *same* direction until you give it another kick. When you change its direction, it does not move in the new direction until you give it a new kick. Its new motion is a combination of the old motion and the motion caused by the new kick. You may need to experiment with dynamic commands for a while before you understand how the dynaturtle works.
To use the dynaturtle, you will need the procedures in this section. Here is the main procedure:

```
TO DT
MOVETURTLE
COMMAND
DT
END
```

The procedure **DT** moves the turtle (if you have given it a kick), checks to see if you've typed a command, and then starts doing **DT** all over again. It keeps running until the procedure is stopped. Here are four other procedures you will need:[2]

```
TO MOVETURTLE
SETXY ( XCOR + :VX ) ( YCOR + :VY )
END

TO COMMAND
MAKE "COM READKEY
IF :COM = "R [RIGHT 30]
IF :COM = "L [LEFT 30]
IF :COM = "K [KICK]
END

TO READKEY
IF KEYP [OUTPUT READCHAR]
OUTPUT "
END

TO KICK
MAKE "VX :VX + SIN HEADING
MAKE "VY :VY + COS HEADING
END
```

To start the dynaturtle, you need a procedure to initialize the dynaturtle's position and velocity:

```
TO STARTUP
CLEARSCREEN
MAKE "VX 0
MAKE "VY 0
END
```

To try out the dynaturtle, type in the Listener window

```
STARTUP
DT
```

At first the turtle will stay at the center of the screen. The **COMMAND** procedure allows three different commands at present. Later you can change them in any way you like.

• If you type **R** the turtle will turn right 30 degrees.

• If you type **L** the turtle will turn left 30 degrees.

---

[2] The **KICK** procedure uses the trigonometric functions **SIN** and **COS** in order to change the turtle's velocity, which can be thought of as a vector (*VX,VY*). This procedure would normally be used by elementary school children as a black box.

• If you type **K** you will give the turtle a *kick* in the direction it is heading.

The turtle will now keep moving in the direction it started until you give it another kick in some direction.

8.3.2. Activities with a Dynaturtle

Start the dynaturtle moving by typing

STARTUP
DT

and then typing the **K** key for "kick."

• Make the dynaturtle move in a different direction by typing the **R** or **L** key.

• Make the dynaturtle move horizontally across the screen.

• Make the dynaturtle go faster.

• Make the dynaturtle go slower, without changing direction.

• Before you start the dynaturtle, draw a marker (a small box or "x") somewhere on the screen. Then start the dynaturtle and see if you can move the turtle to the marker. If the marker is easy for the dynaturtle to get to, move it over a little and try again.

• Start the dynaturtle from the center of the screen. Can you make it stop?

• Draw a circular "racetrack" on the screen and see if you can"drive" the dynaturtle around the track.

• Move the dynaturtle to the marker, and make it stop there.

When you try these activities you may find that some of them are harder than you thought. The problems you have making the dynaturtle do what you want it to do are similar to the problems astronauts would have moving around in outer space, or maneuvering a rocket to connect up with a space platform or land on the moon.

8.3.3. Changing the Dynaturtle's Behavior

After some experimentation with the dynaturtle, you may want to make changes in the dynaturtle procedures. Since changes in the dynaturtle's behavior are controlled by the **COMMAND** procedure, you can start by changing that procedure as follows:

```
TO COMMAND
MAKE "COM READKEY
IF :COM = "R [RIGHT 30]
IF :COM = "L [LEFT 30]
IF :COM = "K [KICK]
END
```

If you like, you can change the *angle* the dynaturtle rotates when you type **R** or **L**, by changing the 30 in **COMMAND** to another number. You could add commands to raise or lower the dynaturtle's pen:

```
IF  :COM = "U  [PENUP]
IF  :COM = "D  [PENDOWN]
```

Your **COMMAND** procedure would now look like this:

```
TO COMMAND
MAKE "COM READKEY
IF :COM = "R [RIGHT 30]
IF :COM = "L [LEFT 30]
IF :COM = "K [KICK]
IF  :COM = "U [PENUP]
IF  :COM = "D [PENDOWN]
END
```

Of course you can change the key names for carrying out the commands by changing the letters on the keyboard. Some people like to have the right and left keys next to each other on the keyboard. If you choose **A** for "left" and **S** for "right," then the **COMMAND** procedure becomes:

```
TO COMMAND
MAKE "COM READKEY
IF :COM = "S [RIGHT 30]
IF :COM = "A [LEFT 30]
IF :COM = "K [KICK]
IF :COM = "U [PENUP]
IF :COM = "D [PENDOWN]
END
```

Another change could be to make the *force* of the kick a variable. If you did this you would have to change the **KICK** procedure and the **STARTUP** procedure as well as **COMMAND**.

```
TO KICK :FORCE
MAKE "VX :VX + :FORCE * ( SIN HEADING )
MAKE "VY :VY + :FORCE * ( COS HEADING )
END
```

You would also have to add a line to STARTUP to set the starting value for the force:

```
TO STARTUP
MAKE "VX 0
MAKE "VY 0
MAKE "FORCE .1
END
```

You can choose any value you want for the starting force.
You would now have to change the KICK line in the **COMMAND** procedure to read

```
IF :COM = "K [KICK :FORCE]
```

Also, you could add two more commands (say, + and −) that increase and decrease the force. The **COMMAND** procedure would now be

```
TO COMMAND
MAKE "COM READKEY
IF :COM = "R [RT 30]
IF :COM = "L [LT 30]
IF :COM = "K [KICK :FORCE]
IF :COM = "U [PENUP]
IF :COM = "D [PENDOWN]
IF :COM = "+ [MAKE "FORCE :FORCE  + .1]
IF :COM = "− [MAKE "FORCE :FORCE  − .1]
END
```

Now try out the dynaturtle with some of these changes, and see what can happen.

Some other possible changes:

- Add a "reverse kick" command that makes the dynaturtle move more slowly.

- Add commands that make the turtle *print* its speed, heading, and kick force.

CHAPTER **9**

Inputs, Outputs, and Recursion

One important difference between Logo and other common programming languages is that, in Logo, words and lists can be used as inputs and outputs to procedures. Therefore, when you program in Logo, you can work in terms of operations that act on entire words and lists, rather than only on individual numbers and characters. Consider the **DOUBLE.LIST** procedure that was introduced in section 5.4:

```
TO DOUBLE.LIST :X
OUTPUT SENTENCE :X :X
END
```

```
PRINT DOUBLE.LIST [DO RE MI]
DO RE MI DO RE MI
```

The importance of making this procedure **OUTPUT** its result is not merely so that you can **PRINT** the result, but so that you can use the result as an input to another procedure that can perform further operations. For instance, if you have an operation **REVERSE.LIST** that reverses a list (as we shall discuss in section 9.1 below) then you can produce the reverse of the double of a list **X** by

REVERSE.LIST DOUBLE.LIST :X

More generally, you can construct complex operations on words and lists as successions of procedures, each of which performs a simple operation and passes the result on to the next procedure. To obtain an operation that removes the last word from a list, reverses what is left, and doubles the result, you can write:

DOUBLE.LIST (REVERSE.LIST (BUTLAST :X))

as in the command

```
PRINT DOUBLE.LIST (REVERSE.LIST (BUTLAST [A B C D]))
C B A C B A
```

which produces the chain of operations shown in figure 9.1. Building up complex operations by combining simpler operations is common programming practice in working with numbers. For example, it is natural to think of computing $(x - 1)^2 + 1$ in terms of the simpler operations of subtracting 1 from a number, squaring the result, and adding 1. Logo enables you to use the same kind of strategy in dealing with words and lists.

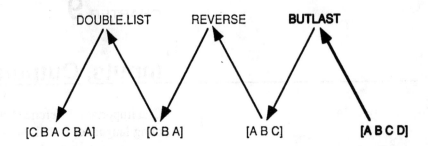

Figure 9.1: Chain of inputs and outputs in a sequence of list operations

The ability to construct complex operations as combinations of simpler ones is particularly powerful when combined with another problem solving strategy: One can often solve a problem by first solving a simpler problem of the same sort and then making a simple modification to the answer. For example, suppose you want to write a procedure that counts the number of words in a list. Imagine that you already know how many words are in the **BUTFIRST** of the list. Then you could solve your original problem by simply taking the number of words in the **BUTFIRST** and adding 1.

Recursive procedures, in general, are the computational analogues of strategies that attack problems by reducing them to simpler problems of the same sort. Given the ability of Logo procedures to manipulate words and lists, this implies that many useful word and list operations can be implemented as surprisingly simple recursive procedures. This chapter examines a few of them. We consider first a number of procedures involved with reversing words and lists and checking for palindromes. Then we discuss operations that select words from lists and test whether a word is a member of a list. Finally, we show how the problem of converting numbers from one base to another can be solved by a simple recursive strategy.

9.1. Reversing Words and Lists

This section shows how to use recursion to write a procedure **REVERSE** that takes a word as input and outputs the word with the characters reversed. That is to say, **REVERSE** behaves as follows:

PRINT REVERSE "STRESSED
DESSERTS

PRINT REVERSE "RUMPLESTILTSKIN
NISKTLITSELPMUR

PRINT REVERSE REVERSE "RUMPLESTILTSKIN
RUMPLESTILTSKIN

Logo's **LAST** and **BUTLAST** operations, which encourage thinking about a word in terms of its last character and the rest of the word, suggest a recursive strategy for implementing the **REVERSE** procedure. It is based on the following idea: suppose you are given a word, say **BIRD**, and you are asked to reverse it. Now imagine that you have somehow managed to generate the reverse of all but the last character of the word—**RIB**. Then all you have to do to reverse the original word is to take the last character, **D**, and place it at the front of what you already have—**DRIB**. This reduces the problem of reversing a word to the problem of reversing a shorter word, namely, the **BUTLAST** of the word. That problem reduces in turn to reversing a still shorter word, namely, the **BUTLAST** of the **BUTLAST**, and so on, with shoter and shorter words. You can diagram this process as follows:

REVERSE "BIRD is **D <–> RIB**

or the last character of **BIRD** added in front of **RIB**. But

RIB is **REVERSE "BIR** which is **R <–> IB**

or the last character of **BIR** added in front of **IB**. But

IB is **REVERSE "BI** which is **I <–> B**

or the last character of **BI** added in front of **B**. Now put all these together:

REVERSE "BIRD
      = **D <–> (REVERSE "BIR)**
      = **D <–> R <–> (REVERSE "BI)**
      = **D <–> R <–> I <–> (REVERSE "B)**
      = **D <–> R <–> I <–> B**

This strategy, reducing the problem of reversing a word to the problem of reversing **BUTLAST** of the word, leads to the following recursive procedure:

```
TO REVERSE :X
OUTPUT WORD (LAST :X) (REVERSE BUTLAST :X)
END
```

However, if you execute this procedure, it will not work. Instead, it produces the error

LAST doesn't like the empty word as input, in REVERSE

The problem is that there is no *stop rule*. Nothing tells **REVERSE** to stop taking **LAST**s and **BUTLAST**s of its input, and Logo finally complains when the procedure attempts to take **LAST** of the empty word. At some point, **REVERSE** should simply output an answer directly without reducing the problem to one of reversing a still shorter word. For example, if the word to be reversed is a single character, then **REVERSE** of the word is the word itself, so you can add to **REVERSE** the stop rule:

IF BUTLAST :X = " [OUTPUT :X]

where **BUTLAST :X** being equal to **:X** signals that **:X** consists of a
single character. So here is the complete procedure:

TO REVWORD :X
IF BUTLAST :X = " [OUTPUT :X]
OUTPUT WORD (LAST :X) (REVERSE BUTLAST :X)
END

An alternative stop rule allows the recursion to proceed one step
further to the point where the input is empty, and then return the
empty word:

TO REVERSE :X
IF :X = " [OUTPUT :X]
OUTPUT WORD (LAST :X) (REVERSE BUTLAST :X)
END

This has the same effect as the previous version, as can be seen by
observing what happens when this procedure is used to reverse a
one-character word:

REVERSE "B = B <–> REVERSE "
$$= B <–> \{empty\}$$
$$= B$$

Figure 9.2: Procedure calls in
evaluating **REVERSE "BIRD**

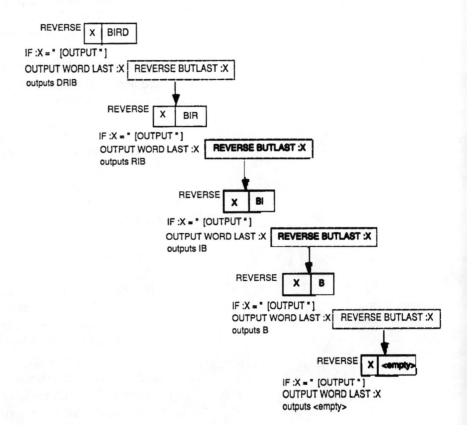

Similar reasoning can be applied to produce a procedure **REVERSE.LIST** that takes a list as input and returns the list of words in reverse order, as in

PRINT REVERSE.LIST [OH SAY CAN YOU SEE]
SEE YOU CAN SAY OH

As before, the problem reduces to combining the **LAST** of the input list with **REVERSE.LIST** of the **BUTLAST**, only, since you will be combining lists rather than words, you should use **SENTENCE** rather than **WORD** to form the combination. The stop rule checks for the list being reduced to the empty, only this time must you check for the empty list rather than the empty word. Here is the procedure:

TO REVERSE.LIST :X
IF :X = [ ] [OUTPUT] [ ]
OUTPUT SENTENCE (LAST :X) (REVERSE.LIST BUTLAST :X)
END

You can combine **REVERSE** and **REVERSE.LIST** to obtain a procedure **REVERSE.ALL** that takes a list as input and returns a list of the words in reverse order, with each word reversed, as well:

PRINT REVERSE.ALL [OH SAY CAN YOU SEE]
EES UOY NAC YAS HO

All you need to do to implement **REVERSE.ALL** is to modify **REVERSE.LIST** so that it **REVERSE**s the **LAST** word of its input before combining that with the result of reversing the **BUTLAST**:

TO REVERSE.ALL :X
IF BUTLAST :X = [ ] [OUTPUT [ ]]
OUTPUT SENTENCE (REVWORD LAST :X)
**   (REVALL BUTLAST :X)**
END

The reasoning that led to these procedures is typical of most recursive procedures that involve words and lists:

- There is a *reduction step* that reduces the problem to a similar problem on a shorter word or list (usually the **BUTFIRST** or **BUTLAST** of the input).

- There is a *stop rule* that checks for some simple case (usually the input being reduced to a single element, or to the empty word or the empty list).[1]

---

[1] Notice that in the actual procedure, the stop rule is written before the reduction step. But when you formulate a recursive solution, you most likely discover the reduction step first and then design an appropriate stop rule.

Finding Palindromes

You can apply **REVERSE** to the problem by checking whether a word is a palindrome, that is, whether the word reads the same backwards as forwards. For example:

```
PRINT PALINDROME? "ABA
TRUE
PRINT PALINDROME? "ABC
FALSE
PRINT PALINDROME? "RACECAR
TRUE
```

Since a word is a palindrome precisely when it is equal to its reverse, you can easily write a Logo predicate that tests for palindromes:[2]

```
TO PALINDROME? :X
IF :X = REVERSE :X [OUTPUT "TRUE]
OUTPUT "FALSE
END
```

One interesting project that involves palindromes has to do with numbers: Start with any integer. If it is a palindrome, then stop. Otherwise add the number to its reverse. If that is a palindrome, then stop, and so on. The question is, if you start with any number, will the process eventually produce a palindrome?

You can write a Logo program to carry out this process:

```
TO MAKE.PALINDROME :NUMBER
PRINT :NUMBER
IF PALINDROME? :NUMBER [STOP]
MAKE.PALINDROME :NUMBER + REVERSE :NUMBER
END
```

```
MAKE.PALINDROME 78
78
165
726
1353
4884
```

```
MAKE.PALINDROME 16793
16793
56554
102119
1013320
1246421
```

---

[2] Notice that since the Logo predicate = itself outputs either **TRUE** or **FALSE**, you can write this same procedure more simply as

```
TO PALINDROME? :X
OUTPUT (:X = REVERSE :X)
END
```

This is a good program to experiment with. As a project, search for numbers less than 1000 that do not seem to produce palindromes in a very few steps.

9.2. Recursive Procedures that Manipulate Lists

Logo's list operations **FIRST**, **LAST**, **BUTFIRST**, and **BUTLAST** are the basic ways to reduce lists to simpler lists. List operations can often be implemented by means of recursive strategies that reduce the problem of performing some operation on a list to the problem of performing a similar operation on the **BUTFIRST** (or **BUTLAST**) of the list. This section considers three useful list operations that are included as primitives in Object Logo:

- **COUNT**, which takes a list as input and returns the number of items in the list

- **ITEM**, which takes a number n and a list as input and returns the nth item of the list

- **MEMBERP**, which takes an item and a list as input and returns **TRUE** or **FALSE**, depending on whether the item is a member of the list

and shows how these can be inplemented in Logo as recursive procedures using **FIRST** and **BUTFIRST**. In order to avoid confusion with the primitive operations, we'll call three corresponding procedures **LENGTH**, **PICK**, and **MEMBER?**.

9.2.1. The LENGTH procedure

The **LENGTH** procedure takes a list as input and outputs the number of items in the list:

```
PRINT LENGTH [HAVE A NICE DAY]
4

PRINT LENGTH [HAVE]
1

PRINT LENGTH [ ]
0
```

The implementation of **LENGTH** uses a simple recursive strtategy:

- The length of a list is 1 plus the length of the **BUTFIRST** of the list.

- The length of the empty list is 0.

That is to say, you can compute the length of a list by first computing the length of the **BUTFIRST** of the list and adding 1 to the result. But computing the length of the **BUTFIRST** reduces to computing the length of a still shorter list, and so on until you are reduced to computing the length of the empty list, which is 0. Here is an example of this process in action:

LENGTH [DO RE MI FA]
= 1 + (LENGTH [RE MI FA])
= 1 + (1 + (LENGTH [MI FA]))
= 1 + (1 + (1 + (LENGTH [FA])))
= 1 + (1 + (1 + (1 + (LENGTH [ ]))))
= 1 + (1 + (1 + (1 + (1 + 0))))
= 1 + (1 + (1 + (1 + 1)))
= 1 + (1 + 2)
= 1 + 3
= 4

Although the process seems complicated when it is "unwound" as in the example above, you can readily express it as a recursive rule:

- *Reduction Step:* Output 1 plus the length of the **BUTFIRST** of the list.

- *Stop Rule:* If the list is empty output 0.

TO LENGTH :X
IF :X = [ ] [OUTPUT 0]
OUTPUT 1 + LENGTH BUTFIRST :X
END

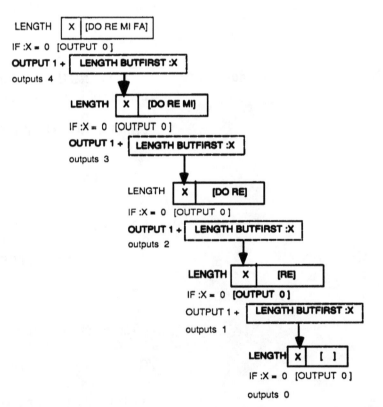

Figure 9.3: Procedure calls in evaluating **LENGTH [DO RE MI FA]**

9.2.2. The PICK procedure

One of the most useful operations to have in working with lists is the ability to select an item from a list. Consider the problem of writing a procedure **PICK** that takes a number and a list as inputs and outputs the designated item from the list: If the number is 1, **PICK** outputs the first item in the list; if the number is 2, **PICK** outputs the second item in the list; and so on.

There is a recursive strategy for computing **PICK** in terms of the operations **FIRST** and **BUTFIRST**. You can reduce the problem of picking an item from a list to the problem of picking an item from the **BUTFIRST** of the list: The nth item of a list is the same as the $(n-1)$st item of the **BUTFIRST** of the list. The recursive plan is:

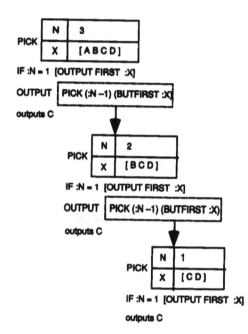

- *Reduction Step:* To **PICK** the n item from a list, then **PICK** the $(n-1)$st item of the **BUTFIRST** of the list.

- *Stop Rule:* If $n=1$ then output the **FIRST** item in the list.

This strategy can be expressed as the following Logo procedure:

```
TO PICK :N :X
IF :N = 1 [OUTPUT FIRST :X]
OUTPUT PICK (:N – 1) (BUTFIRST :X)
END
```

Figure 9.4 shows the chain of procedure calls and the inputs and outputs in evaluating:

PICK 3 [A B C D]

where picking the 3rd item of **[A B C D]** reduces to the picking the 2nd item of **[B C D]** which reduces to picking the 1st item of **[C D]**, which is **C**.[3]

Figure 9.4: Procedure calls in evaluating PICK 3 [A B C D]

9.2.3. The MEMBER? Predicate

The final operation we shall discuss is the **MEMBER?** predicate, which takes a word and a list as inputs and checks whether the word is a member of the list, outputting **TRUE** or **FALSE** accordingly. The recursive strategy here is that it is easy to check if the desired word is the **FIRST** item in the list. If it is, then **MEMBER?** should output **TRUE**. If not, you check to see if the word is in **BUTFIRST** of the list, and so on. If the list ever becomes empty, you have run out of elements to check the word against, so **MEMBER?** should output **FALSE**. The resulting procedure is

---

[3] If you call **PICK** with **N** larger than the length of the list, then the procedure signals an error. For example, trying to pick the 5th item of **[A B C D]** reduces to the 4th item of **[B C D]**, the 3rd item of **[C D]**, the 2nd item of **[D]**, and finally **PICK** is called with **N** equal to 1 and **X** equal to the empty list. At this point **PICK** tries to compute **FIRST** of **X**. This signals an error, since **FIRST** does not operate on the empty list.

```
TO MEMBER? :WORD :LIST
IF :LIST = [ ] [OUTPUT "FALSE]
IF :WORD = (FIRST :LIST) [OUTPUT "TRUE]
OUTPUT MEMBER? :WORD (BUTFIRST :LIST)
END
```

Converting to Pig Latin

As an example of using **MEMBER?** and recursion, you can write a program that converts a sentence to Pig Latin. For each word in the sentence, you must move the leading consonants to the end of the word and add on "ay" as in

Isthay entencesay isay inay igpay atinlay.

Since you need to strip off consonants, it is useful to have a predicate that checks whether a word begins with a vowel. That's easily done:

```
TO BEGINS.WITH.VOWEL? :W
OUTPUT MEMBER? (FIRST :W) [A E I O U]
END
```

Notice that this outputs **TRUE** or **FALSE** because **MEMBER?** outputs **TRUE** or **FALSE**.
Here's a program that converts a single word to pig Latin:

```
TO PIG :W
TEST BEGINS.WITH.VOWEL? :W
IFTRUE [OUTPUT WORD :W "AY]
IFFALSE [OUTPUT PIG WORD (BUTFIRST :W) (FIRST :W)]
END
```

The cleverness in **PIG** is the recursive call that ensures that **PIG** will keep stripping letters off the front of the word until it reaches a vowel. To better understand this point, you should draw a diagram that gives the sequence of recursive calls in computing ,

```
PRINT PIG "STRING
INGSTRAY
```

Now, if you work word by word, you can convert an entire sentence. The trick is to think recursively again:

```
TO PIGL :S
IF :S = [ ] [OUTPUT [ ]]
OUTPUT SENTENCE (PIG FIRST :S) (PIGL BUTFIRST :S)
END
```

PRINT PIGL [THIS IS ANOTHER RECURSIVE PROCEDURE]
ISTHAY ISAY ANOTHERAY ECURSIVERAY OCEDUREPRAY

The strategy used in **PIGL** is a standard way to "do something to every item in a list." The idea is to reason as follows. Suppose you have already converted the words in the **BUTFIRST** of the list. Then you need only **SENTENCE** this with the result of converting the first word in the list, and you are done. In this way, the problem of converting the entire list reduces to converting **BUTFIRST** of the list, which reduces to **BUTFIRST** of *that* list, and so on, and so on. Finally the problem is reduced to that of converting the empty list, for which the answer is empty.

9.3. Radix Conversion

As a final example of a problem that seems difficult but has a simple recursive solution, we consider the problem of converting an integer written in base 10 notation to some other base, say, base 8. For instance, we would like to find that 65 base ten is written as 101 in base 8, 100 base ten is 144 base 8, 1000 base 10 is 1750 base 8, and so on.

There is a clever recursive strategy for solving this problem. Suppose that n is some integer and that you want to find the string of digits that represents n in base 8. Think about what such a representation means. For example, to say that 100 base ten is written as 144 base 8 means that

$$100 = 1 \times 8 \times 8 + 4 \times 8 + 4 = 144 \text{ base } 8$$

The key insight is that it is easy to find the *last* digit of the string of digits that represents n: This is just the remainder when n is divided by 8:

REMAINDER 100 8 is 4

Now suppose you take the string of digits that represents n and strip off the last digit. In terms of base 8 representation, that corresponds to shifting everything one place to the right and dropping the last digit. But this corresponds precisely to dividing the number by 8 and dropping the remainder. That is to say, if you take the string of digits that represents n in base 8 and leave off the last digit, what you are left with is the string of digits that represents the integer quotient of n by 8, written in base 8:

INQUOTIENT 100 8 is 12, and 12 represented in base 8 is 14, which is all but the last digit if 144.

So now you have a simple description of the string of digits that represents n in base 8

- The last digit is the remainder of n by 8.

- The **BUTLAST** of the string is the base 8 representation of integer quotient of n by 8.

So the problem of representing n in base 8 reduces to representing the quotient of n by 8 in base 8, which reduces further, and so on. The reductions stop when you reach a quotient that is less than 8, which is represented in base 8 as a single digit.

So here is how to generate n in base 8:

- **If n is = 0 the result is 0.**

- **Otherwise**
  * Find the digits that represent the quotient of n by 8, and

  * append to these the remainder of n divided by 8.

Using the Logo **WORD** operation to glue numbers together, this strategy translates into the procedure:

```
TO BASE8 :N
IF :N = 0 [OUTPUT 0]
OUTPUT WORD
_ (BASE8 (INTQUOTIENT :N 8))
_ (REMAINDER :N 8)
END
```

The only slight bug in this procedure is that it generates an extra zero to the left of each non-zero number. You can fix this by providing another procedure to remove the extra zero:

```
TO CONVERT.TO.BASE.8 :N
IF :N = :0 [OUTPUT 0]
OUTPUT BUTFIRST BASE8 :N
END
```

Of course, there is nothing special about base 8. You can convert to any base less than 10 in the same way.

```
TO CONVERT :N :B
IF :N = :0 [OUTPUT 0]
OUTPUT BUTFIRST (BASE :N :B)
END
```

```
TO BASE :N :B
IF :N = 0 [OUTPUT 0]
OUTPUT WORD
_ (BASE (INTQUOTIENT :N :B) :B)
_ (REMAINDER :N :B)
END
```

For example

PRINT CONVERT 1000 2
1111101000

For bases larger than 10, you can use the same strategy, except that you will need "digits" to represent the single-digit numbers larger than 10. For instance, in base 16 you can represent 10 by the letter A and 11 by the letter B, and so on.[4]

So you can represent single digit numbers in base 16 by using the following procedure:

```
TO DIG :N
!IF :N < 10 [OUTPUT :N]
IF :N = 10 [OUTPUT "A]
IF :N = 11 [OUTPUT "B]
IF :N = 12 [OUTPUT "C]
IF :N = 13 [OUTPUT "D]
IF :N = 14 [OUTPUT "E]
IF :N = 15 [OUTPUT "F]
END
```

Then a procedure for printing numbers in bases up to 16 could use:

```
TO CONVERT :N :B
IF :B > 16 [PRINT [ERROR :BASE TOO LARGE]
IF :N = 0 [OUTPUT 0]
OUTPUT BUTFIRST BASE :N :B
END
```

```
TO BASE :N :B
IF :N = 0 [OUTPUT 0]
OUTPUT WORD
_ (BASE (INTQUOTIENT :N :B) :B)
_ (DIG (REMAINDER :N :B))
END
```

PRINT CONVERT 20000 16
4E20

PRINT CONVERT 20000 12
B6A8

---

[4] This is the "hexadecimal" notation commonly used for specifying computer memory addresses.

CHAPTER **10**

Advanced Use of Lists

We've seen how words can be grouped together into Logo lists. But lists in Logo can be used for more than just collecting words. For example, the random sentence generator of section 6.2 picked its nouns from a list:

MAKE "NOUNS [DOGS CATS CHILDREN TIGERS]

Suppose, however, you want to make sentences using "nouns" that aren't single words. For example, you may want to make sentences about dogs, cats, children, tigers, and pack rats. You can't do this by adding the two words **PACK RATS** to the above list as in

MAKE "NOUNS
_   **[DOGS CATS CHILDREN TIGERS PACK RATS]**

because making a sentence whose nouns are words picked at random from this list of 6 items would give results including things like

PACK LAUGH
RATS RUN

.

What you need to do is to take the two words **PACK RATS** and group these together as a *single* item within the list of nouns. You can do this in Logo by

MAKE "NOUNS
_   **[DOGS CATS CHILDREN TIGERS [PACK RATS]]**

What you have now is a list of five items. The first four items in the list are words: **DOGS, CATS, CHILDREN, TIGERS**. The fifth item in the list is *itself* a list **[PACK RATS]** consisting of two words, **PACK** and **RATS**. When you pick items from the list **NOUNS**, you may get a single word like **DOGS**, or you may get the two-word list **[PACK RATS]**. This new value of **NOUNS** gives the desired results in the sentence generating program of section 6.2:

DOGS BITE
PACK RATS LAUGH
.

The general point here is that in Logo *the items in a list can be, not only words, but also other lists.*

10.1 Hierarchical Structures

If you think of a list of words as a simple list (or one-level list), then the **NOUNS** list above can be considered to be a two-level list, that is, a list with an element that is itself a list. But there is no reason to stop there. In general, you can have lists whose items are themselves lists whose items are lists, and so on. And this general notion of a list in Logo provides lots of power and flexibility in dealing with complex structures. For example, figure 10.1 shows a *tree structure* that represents part of the organization of the U.S. government.

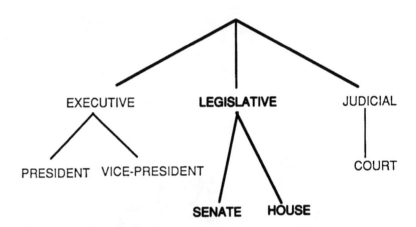

Figure 10.1: Hierarchical organization of the U.S. Government

From our point of view, the important thing about this structure is that it is a *hierarchy*, that is, it consists of parts that themselves consist of parts, and so on. You can represent the tree structure in figure 10.1 as the Logo list

**[[EXECUTIVE [PRESIDENT VICE-PRESIDENT]]
[LEGISLATIVE [SENATE HOUSE]]
[JUDICIAL [COURT]]]**

This is a list of three items. The first item, which is the list

[EXECUTIVE [PRESIDENT VICE-PRESIDENT]]

is itself a list of two items, of which the first is the word **EXECUTIVE** and the second is a list of two words, and so on.

Logo's use of lists is adapted from the programming language Lisp, which was developed for research in artificial intelligence. Lists have proved to be indispensable in programs that deal with symbol manipulation and complex data structures, and their presence in Logo and Lisp is largely responsible for the fact that programming in these languages is very different from working in languages like

BASIC and Fortran. In those languages, complex data structures must be encoded in terms of numbers, character strings, and arrays. Lists, however, allow many kinds of complex hierarchical structures to be represented directly, and therefore lists play a major role in computer applications dealing with complex data structures. In particular, they are the workhorse of most programs that are heavily involved with symbolic expressions, rather than just numerical data. The projects in the section 10.3 illustrate how lists are used in this way. However, this hardly scratches the surface of what can be done. The book by Winston and Horn [32] provides many examples of the uses of lists in symbol manipulation, in the context of the language Lisp.

10.1.1. List Operations

We've already seen how to use the Logo operations **FIRST**, **LAST**, **BUTFIRST**, **BUTLAST**, and **SENTENCE** for working with "simple" lists of words. These same operations extend to work with complex lists, as well. For example, suppose you create a complicated list:

MAKE "TRY [[A B C] D [E F]]

TRY is a list of three items, the list **[A BC]**, the word **D**, and the list **[E F]**.

PRINT :TRY
[A B C] D [E F]

Note how **TRY** is printed. Logo always prints lists without the outermost pair of brackets.

The operations **FIRST** and **LAST** output, as usual, the first and last items in a list. In a complex list these items may themselves be lists:

PRINT FIRST :TRY
A B C
PRINT LAST :TRY
E F

BUTFIRST outputs the list consisting of all elements but the first, and **BUTLAST** outputs the list consisting of all elements but the last:

PRINT BUTFIRST :TRY
D [E F]
PRINT BUTLAST :TRY
[A B C] D

Keep in mind that these operations output, in general, new lists to which you can apply further operations. For example,

FIRST FIRST :TRY

is the first item of the first item of **TRY**, which is the first item of **[A B C]**, which is **A**.

FIRST LAST :TRY

is the first item of the last item of **TRY**, which is the first item of **[E F]**, which is **E**.

FIRST BUTFIRST :TRY

is the first item of the **BUTFIRST** of **TRY**, which is the first item of **[D [E F]]**, which is **D**. (In general, **FIRST** of **BUTFIRST** of any list is the second item of the list.)

FIRST BUTFIRST LAST :TRY

is the **FIRST** of the **BUTFIRST** of the **LAST** of **TRY**, which is the **FIRST** of the **BUTFIRST** of **[E F]**, which is **F**.

The four operations **FIRST**, **LAST**, **BUTFIRST**, and **BUTLAST** are used for extracting pieces of lists. To combine lists into more complex lists, we have the Logo operation **LIST**. **LIST** takes a collection of inputs and outputs a list whose items are those inputs. For example, if there are three inputs, the word **XX**, the word **YY**, and the list **[A B C]**, **LIST** outputs the list of those three items:

```
PRINT (LIST "XX "YY [A B C])
XX YY [A B C]
```

If, instead of the word **XX** and the word **YY**, you use the lists **[XX]** and **[YY]**, then **LIST** outputs a list whose first and second items are those lists:

```
PRINT (LIST [XX] [YY] [A B C])
[XX] [YY] [A B C]
```

As another example, you can construct the list **TRY** used above as

```
(LIST [A B C] "D [E F])
```

or a more complex list, such as the U.S. Government list of the previous section as:

```
MAKE "EX [EXECUTIVE [PRESIDENT VICE-PRESIDENT]]
MAKE "LEG [LEGISLATIVE [SENATE HOUSE]]
MAKE "JUD [JUDICIAL [COURT]]
MAKE "GOV (LIST :EX :LEG :LUD)
```

Another way to combine items into a list is by means of the **FPUT** operation. **FPUT** takes two inputs, of which the second must be a list. It puts its first input at the beginning of its second input, that is, it outputs a list whose **FIRST** is the first input and whose **BUTFIRST** is the second input:

PRINT FPUT "A [D E F]
A D E F
PRINT FPUT [A] [D E F]
[A] D E F
PRINT FPUT [A B C] [D E F]
[A B C] D E F

    LPUT is similar to **FPUT**, except that it installs its first input as the *last* item in the list:

PRINT LPUT "A [D E F]
D E F A
PRINT LPUT [A] [D E F]
D E F [A]
PRINT LPUT [A B C] [D E F]
D E F [A B C]

    The Logo operation **SENTENCE**, which we previously used to combine words into lists, can also be used with more complex lists. If **SENTENCE** is given a number of lists as inputs, it combines all of the elements of these lists into a single list:

PRINT SENTENCE [A [B C]] [D E F]
A [B C] D E F

Be careful about the distinction between **LIST** and **SENTENCE**. Compare the example just above with

PRINT LIST [A [B C]] [D E F]
[A [B C]] [D E F]

    This description of **SENTENCE** makes sense only when all of the inputs to **SENTENCE** are themselves lists. In order to make this consistent with our previous definition of **SENTENCE** for combining words into lists we extend the definition as follows: if one of the inputs to **SENTENCE** is a word, then you replace that word by the one-item list containing that word, and then apply the definition of **SENTENCE** given above. For example:[1]

(SENTENCE "A "B "C)

gives the same result as

(SENTENCE [A] [B] [C])

which is the list **[A B C]**.

---

[1] If you are interested only in combining words into lists to be printed (as in most elementary Logo programs), then **SENTENCE** is the only operation you need for constructing lists. However, when you are interested in using lists as hierarchical data structures, you need the finer control provided by **FPUT**, **LPUT**, and **LIST**. For example, it is always true that **:X** is the first item of **FPUT :X :Y**. But this is not the case with **SENTENCE**. For instance, if **:X** is **[A B C]** and **:Y** is **[D E]**, then the first item of **SENTENCE :X :Y** is the word **A**.

SENTENCE "A [B [C D]]

gives the same result as

SENTENCE [A] [B [C D]]

which is the list **[A B [C D]]**. In general, **SENTENCE** and **LIST** give the same result if all the inputs are words.

10.1.2. Example: Association Lists

One particularly simple form of list is a list of pairs, which can be used to represent simple tables in which values are associated to things:

```
MAKE "TABLE1
_  [ [COLOR PURPLE]
_    [SIZE HUGE]
_    [WEIGHT [1 TON]]]
```

Such a list of pairs is called an *association list*. The first item in each pair is referred to as the *key* and second item is the corresponding *value*. The most important function for operating on tables represented as association lists is **LOOKUP**, which outputs the value corresponding to a given key:

```
PRINT LOOKUP "SIZE :TABLE1
HUGE
```

LOOKUP is implemented by means of an auxiliary function called **ENTRY**, which outputs the pair in which the key occurs, or outputs the empty list if there is no such pair in the table. **LOOKUP** then outputs the second item in the **ENTRY**, or signals an error if the key was not found. **ENTRY** is implemented by scanning down the list in the usual fashion:[2]

```
TO ENTRY :KEY :TABLE
IF :TABLE = [ ] [OUTPUT [ ]]
IF :KEY = (FIRST FIRST :TABLE) [OUTPUT (FIRST :TABLE)]
OUTPUT ENTRY :KEY (BUTFIRST :TABLE)
END
```

LOOKUP is implemented as

```
TO LOOKUP :KEY :TABLE
MAKE "PAIR ENTRY :KEY :TABLE
IF NOT (:PAIR = [ ]) [OUTPUT LAST :PAIR]
PRINT [ERROR: KEY NOT IN TABLE]
TOPLEVEL
END
```

---

[2] This is very similar to the **MEMBER?** procedure in section 9.2.3.

The **TOPLEVEL** command used by **LOOKUP** stops the evaluation of a Logo program and returns command to the user. It is used here to stop the entire program (not just **LOOKUP**) when **LOOKUP** signals an error.

Another use for association lists that arises in symbol manipulation is for substituting values from a table. The following **SUBST** procedure takes a list and a table as inputs. For each item in the list that is a key in the table, it replaces the key by the corresponding value. For example, with **TABLE1** as above, you would have:

```
PRINT SUBST [HE IS COLOR AND WEIGHS WEIGHT]
            :TABLE1
HE IS PURPLE AND WEIGHS [1 TON]
```

To define **SUBST**, we'll begin by writing a procedure **SUBST.ITEM** that takes an item and a table as input. If the item is a key in the table then **SUBST.ITEM** outputs the associated value. Otherwise it outputs the original item. Notice that this is almost the same as **LOOKUP** except that it returns the original item instead of signaling an error if the item is not in the table.

```
TO SUBST.ITEM :ITEM :TABLE
MAKE "SUBST.PAIR (ENTRY :ITEM :TABLE)
IF :SUBST.PAIR = [ ] [OUTPUT :ITEM]
OUTPUT LAST :SUBST.PAIR
END
```

The **SUBST** procedure itself is implemented by performing **SUBST.ITEM** on each item in the list, and outputting the list of the results:

```
TO SUBST :LIST :TABLE
IF :LIST = [ ] [OUTPUT [ ]]
OUTPUT FPUT (SUBST.ITEM (FIRST :LIST) :TABLE)
             (SUBST (BUTFIRST :LIST) :TABLE)
END
```

Properties

One way to think of an association list is as a collection of the attributes, or "properties," of some object:

```
MAKE "SUPERGRAPE
     [[COLOR PURPLE] [SIZE HUGE] [WEIGHT [1 TON]]]
```

These attributes can be recovered by using the **LOOKUP** procedure given above. More abstractly, we can forget about the list of pairs, and think in terms of a procedure **PUTPROP**, which associates a given property value to a given symbol. For example,

PUTPROP "SUPER.GRAPE "COLOR "PURPLE

would associate to the symbol **SUPER.GRAPE** a **COLOR** property whose value is **PURPLE**. A corresponding procedure **GETPROP** is used to retrieve a property value, so that, for example,

GETPROP "SUPER.GRAPE "COLOR

would return **PURPLE**. A typical program that uses properties to manage information might contain a line such as

```
PRINT (SENTENCE
_  [THE COLOR OF]
_  :ITEM
_  [IS]
_  (GETPROP :ITEM "COLOR))
```

   PUTPROP and **GETPROP** are readily implemented in terms of association lists, but in some applications, it is better to use other methods for representing properties. In particular, if there are many attributes in a table, performing a **LOOKUP** will be slow, due to the need to scan a long list. Object Logo includes **PUTPROP** and **GETPROP** as primitives, so that you can avoid the need to use long lists to implement tables. In addition, there are primitives **REMPROP**, which takes a symbol and a property name and removes the corresponding property from the symbol, and **PLIST**, which takes a symbol as input and returns a list of that symbol's properties, together with their corresponding values.

10.2. Programs as Data

   One important kind of hierarchical structure that arises in programming is the structure of a program itself. A Logo procedure can be thought of as a list of lines each of which is a list of words. Using Logo lists, you can write *programs* that manipulate other programs. The basic Logo primitives that enable you to do this are **RUN**, which evaluates a list as a Logo command line; **DEFINE**, which constructs a procedure from list data; and **TEXT**, which outputs the representation of a procedure. This section explains how these operations work in the context of an extended example—increasing the capabilities of the simple **INSTANT** program that was introduced in section 8.2.1.

10.2.1. The RUN Command

   The Logo command **RUN** takes a Logo list as input, and evaluates the list as if the list were a command line typed at the keyboard. For example

```
RUN [PRINT [HELLO THERE]
HELLO THERE
RUN LIST "PRINT [HELLO THERE]
HELLO THERE
MAKE "COMMAND "PRINT
MAKE "INPUT [HELLO THERE]
RUN LIST :COMMAND :INPUT
HELLO THERE
```

Example: extending the INSTANT program

One situation in which **RUN** is useful is where you want to build up a list of commands to be evaluated later. As an example, consider the **INSTANT** program of section 8.2.1:

```
TO INSTANT
COMMAND
INSTANT
END

TO COMMAND
MAKE "COM READCHAR
IF :COM = "F [FORWARD 10]
IF :COM = "R [RIGHT 30]
IF :COM = "L [LEFT 30 ]
IF :COM = "C [CLEARSCREEN]
END
```

Suppose you want to add an "undo" feature to the system. That is, typing **F**, **L**, and **R** at the keyboard will cause the turtle to move forward, left, and right as before. In addition, typing **U** will cause the turtle to undo its previous move.

You can implement the undo operation is as follows. As the user of the **INSTANT** system gives commands by pressing the keys, the **INSTANT** program will not only move the turtle, but will also *remember* the turtle motions that were done by saving them in a list. Then, when the user wishes to undo the last command, **INSTANT** will clear the screen, remove the last command from the list, and reprocess the remaining commands.[3]

To implement this strategy let's assume you store the turtle commands in a list called **HISTORY**. For example, if the user types **F** and then **R**, **HISTORY** will be

```
[[FORWARD 10] [RIGHT 30]]
```

Notice that **HISTORY** is a list of lists, in which each entry is the Logo command that should be run to cause the appropriate turtle motion.

The main operation needed now is to take a turtle command and not only do it, but also add it to the **HISTORY** list. This can be accomplished by

```
TO RUN.AND.RECORD :ACTION
RUN :ACTION
MAKE "HISTORY (LPUT :ACTION :HISTORY)    .
END
```

---

[3] There are of course many other ways to implement the undo operation. One advantage of the way chosen here is that it extends nicely to allowing the user of the **INSTANT** system user to define programs, as we shall see in section 10.2.2.

You use **LPUT** to add the new command as the *last* item in **HIS-TORY**.

You now change the **COMMAND** procedure to **RUN.AND.RECORD** the appropriate response to each key:

```
TO COMMAND
MAKE "COM READCHAR
IF :COM = "F [RUN.AND.RECORD [FORWARD 10]]
IF :COM = "R [RUN.AND.RECORD [RIGHT 30]]
IF :COM = "L [RUN.AND.RECORD [LEFT 30]]
IF :COM = "C [RUN.AND.RECORD [CLEARSCREEN]]
END
```

Now, to undo the last command, you remove the last item from **HISTORY**, clear the screen, and run the rest of the commands:

```
TO UNDO
IF :HISTORY = [ ] [STOP]
MAKE "HISTORY BUTLAST :HISTORY
CLEARSCREEN
RUN.ALL :HISTORY
END
```

Note the first line of **UNDO**, which says that if the **HISTORY** list is empty, there is nothing to undo. Also note that with this implementation, repeatedly executing **UNDO** keeps removing more and more items from **HISTORY**, starting with the last one, the one before that, and so on.

The subprocedure **RUN.ALL** takes a list of commands as input and runs all the commands in the list in sequence. (Each command in the list must itself be a list.) **RUN.ALL** uses a recursive strategy. It **RUN**s the first command in the list and then processes the **BUTFIRST** of the list.

```
TO RUN.ALL :COMMANDS
IF :COMMANDS = [ ] [STOP]
RUN FIRST :COMMANDS
RUN.ALL (BUTFIRST :COMMANDS)
END
```

Now all you need to do is add a line to the **COMMAND** procedure so that pressing **U** causes an **UNDO** operation:

```
TO COMMAND
MAKE "COM READCHAR
IF :COM = "F [RUN.AND.RECORD [FORWARD 10]]
IF :COM = "R [RUN.AND.RECORD [RIGHT 30]]
IF :COM = "L [RUN.AND.RECORD [LEFT 30]]
IF :COM = "C [RUN.AND.RECORD [CLEARSCREEN]]
IF :COM = "U [UNDO]
END
```

The complete **INSTANT** program now simply clears the screen and repeatedly calls **COMMAND**. You must also initialize **HISTORY** to be empty:

```
TO SETUP
MAKE "HISTORY [ ]
CLEARSCREEN
INSTANT
END

TO INSTANT
COMMAND
INSTANT
END
```

10.2.2. The DEFINE Command

In addition to using Logo list operations to generate individual command lines that can be **RUN**, you can also write procedures that define other procedures. This is done with the **DEFINE** command. **DEFINE** takes two inputs. This first is the name of the procedure to be defined. The second input is a list of lists organized as follows. The first sublist gives the inputs to the new procedure, and there is one additional sublist for each procedure line. For example

```
DEFINE "TRY [[X Y][PRINT :X][PRINT :Y]]
PO "TRY
TO TRY :X :Y
PRINT :X
PRINT :Y
END

DEFINE "GREET [[ ] [PRINT [HELLO]]]
PO "GREET
TO GREET
PRINT [HELLO]
END
```

Observe that if the procedure is to have no inputs (as in **GREET** above), the **DEFINE** list must include an initial empty list for the input specification. Note also that there is no **END** included in the list of procedure lines.

Example: another extension to INSTANT

Most of the time, of course, you use **TO** rather than **DEFINE** to create Logo procedures. **DEFINE** is reserved for those situations in which you want procedure definition to happen under program control. As an example of this, we'll consider another extension to the **INSTANT** system of section 10.2.1. This time, we'll allow the user of **INSTANT** to name drawings and to recall them by name. For example, we may use the letter **S** for saving drawings. Typing **S** (for "save") will cause the program to ask the user for a name for the drawing. Later on, the user can ask for a previous drawing to be reshown, say by typing **P** for "picture." More than one drawing can be saved at once, each with its own name.

You can implement this is by having the **INSTANT** system save a drawing by *defining the drawing as a procedure*, using the name chosen by the user. The list of lines in the procedure is precisely the **HISTORY** list that you have been using to keep track of what is on the screen. Here is the procedure that implements this "learning" process:

```
TO LEARN
PRINT [WHAT DO YOU WANT TO CALL THIS PICTURE?]
MAKE "NAME READWORD
DEFINE :NAME (FPUT [ ] :HISTORY)
SETUP
END
```

Note that the second input given to **DEFINE** is **FPUT [ ] :HISTORY**, since you need to include an empty input list for the procedure being defined. **LEARN** calls **SETUP** to clear the screen and reinitialize **HISTORY** to prepare for a new drawing.

The behavior of **LEARN** is now:

```
WHAT DO YOU WANT TO CALL THIS PICTURE?
BOX
```

and there is now a procedure called **BOX**, which, when run, draws the picture that currently appears on the screen.

Now you must add a command that asks for an input line and runs it. This is accomplished by

```
TO SHOW.PICTURE
PRINT [WHAT PICTURE DO YOU WANT TO SHOW?]
RUN.AND.RECORD READLIST
END
```

Notice that the input **READLIST** line is both run and recorded. Note also that *any* Logo command could be input and evaluated, not just a call to a procedure created by **LEARN**.

Finally, you must add the appropriate lines to the **COMMAND** procedure so that it will recognize the characters **S** (for save) and **P** (for picture) and run the appropriate procedures.

The complete INSTANT system

Here is a complete listing of the **INSTANT** system developed in the preceding sections:

```
TO SETUP
MAKE "HISTORY [ ]
CLEARSCREEN
INSTANT
END
```

```
TO INSTANT
COMMAND
INSTANT
END

TO COMMAND
MAKE "COM READCHAR
IF :COM = "F [RUN.AND.RECORD [FORWARD 10]]
IF :COM = "R [RUN.AND.RECORD [RIGHT 30]]
IF :COM = "L [RUN.AND.RECORD [LEFT 30]]
IF :COM = "C [RUN.AND.RECORD [CLEARSCREEN]]
IF :COM = "U [UNDO]
END

TO RUN.AND.RECORD :ACTION
RUN :ACTION
MAKE "HISTORY (LPUT :ACTION :HISTORY)
END

TO UNDO
IF :HISTORY = [ ] [STOP]
MAKE "HISTORY BUTLAST :HISTORY
CLEARSCREEN
RUN.ALL :HISTORY
END

TO RUN.ALL :COMMANDS
IF :COMMANDS = [ ] [STOP]
RUN FIRST :COMMANDS
RUN.ALL (BUTFIRST :COMMANDS)
END

TO LEARN
PRINT [WHAT DO YOU WANT TO CALL THIS PICTURE?]
MAKE "NAME READWORD
DEFINE :NAME (FPUT [ ] :HISTORY)
SETUP
END

TO SHOW.PICTURE
PRINT [WHAT PICTURE DO YOU WANT TO SHOW?]
RUN.AND.RECORD READLIST
END
```

There are many possible modifications and improvements to this system. For a good exercise in manipulating lists, consider the following problem. A typical **HISTORY** list to be assembled into a procedure might look like

```
FORWARD 10
RIGHT 30
LEFT 30
FORWARD 10
RIGHT 30
RIGHT 30
```

```
RIGHT 30
FORWARD 10
FORWARD 10
```

It would be nice if, before the **HISTORY** list is made into a procedure, it could be "compressed" so that the procedure that is defined would consist of the command sequence

```
FORWARD 20
RIGHT 90
FORWARD 20
```

Write a procedure **COMPRESS** that will perform this kind of transformation on a list of turtle commands. Once you have **COMPRESS**, the **LEARN** procedure can be rewritten as:

```
TO LEARN
PRINT [WHAT DO YOU WANT TO CALL THIS PICTURE?]
MAKE "NAME READWORD
DEFINE :NAME (FPUT [ ] (COMPRESS :HISTORY))
SETUP
END
```

10.2.3. The TEXT Command

In some instances, it is useful to have an "inverse operation" to **DEFINE,** that is, to be able to take a procedure that is already defined and to extract the text of the procedure so that it can be manipulated as a list. This is done with the Logo command **TEXT**, which takes a procedure name as input and outputs the text of the procedure in the same format as is used in **DEFINE.**
For example, assume that **CORNER** is defined as

```
TO CORNER :A :B
FORWARD :A
RIGHT :B
END
```

Then **TEXT "CORNER** is the list

```
[[:A :B] [FORWARD :A] [RIGHT :B]]
```

Using **TEXT,** you can write procedures that examine and manipulate other procedures.

10.3. More Projects Using Lists

This section presents two open-ended projects that make use of Logo's capability to manipulate lists. The first project is a highly simplified version of a famous program called **DOCTOR** that was developed in the early 1960's by Joseph Weizenbaum. The Logo implementation here uses the association list mechanism that was explained in section 10.1.2. The second program is a Logo version of a well-known computer "learning" program called **ANIMAL,** which demonstrates how to use hierarchical list structures to keep track of information.

10.3.1. Example: The DOCTOR Program

The **DOCTOR** program engages in a "conversation" with the computer user, in which it mimics a nondirective style of psychotherapy. Here is a sample conversation:[4]

DOCTOR
WHAT SEEMS TO BE THE PROBLEM

EVERYONE HATES ME
YOU SAY EVERYONE HATES YOU

WHENEVER I ENTER A ROOM NO ONE WILL LOOK ME IN THE EYE
MANY PEOPLE HAVE THE SAME SORTS OF FEELINGS

THEY LAUGH AT ME BEHIND MY BACK
YOU SEEM TO THINK THEY LAUGH AT YOU BEHIND YOUR BACK

EVEN MY MOTHER HATES ME
YOU FEEL THAT EVEN YOUR MOTHER HATES YOU

EVEN WHEN I WAS A BABY SHE SAID I WAS ALWAYS BAD
PLEASE CONTINUE

How the DOCTOR program works

Although at first glance, the **DOCTOR** program seems to understand and reply to the user's remarks, in reality it is doing nothing of the sort. In fact, the program has two simple methods for generating a response. The first method is to ignore what the user types and simply respond with some sort of hedge like **PLEASE CONTINUE** or **MANY PEOPLE HAVE THE SAME SORTS OF FEELINGS**. The second method involves taking the user's reply, changing some common words like "I," "me," and "am" to the corresponding second person words and appending the transformed response to some qualifying phrase such as **YOU SAY** or **YOU SEEM TO THINK**. The program chooses one of these methods at random for each response.

We'll examine these two methods in turn. The first is very simple. What the program prints is just a phrase picked at random from a suitable list of hedges such as

```
MAKE "HEDGES
_ [[PLEASE GO ON]
_ [PLEASE CONTINUE]
_ [MANY PEOPLE HAVE THE SAME SORTS OF FEELINGS]]
```

---

[4] In order to simplify the program all punctuation has been omitted.

Then the part of the program that implements the first method is just [5]

```
TO HEDGE
PRINT PICKRANDOM :HEDGES
END
```

The second method is more complicated. You must take the user's typed in response, change the "I" words to the corresponding "you" words and append this to a randomly selected qualifier. To perform the "I-you" change, you can use the **SUBST** procedure from section 10.1.2, where the substitution **TABLE** of pairs is made up of first-person pronouns and their second-person counterparts:

```
MAKE "PRONOUNS
_    [[I YOU] [ME YOU] [MY YOUR] [AM ARE]]
```

```
TO CHANGE.PERSON :PHRASE
OUTPUT SUBST :PHRASE :PRONOUNS
END
```

So if the collection of qualifiers is given by

```
MAKE "QUALIFY
_  [[YOU SEEM TO THINK]
_   [YOU FEEL THAT]
_   [YOU SAY]]
```

then the second type of response to the user's input is generated by

```
TO RESPOND :USER.INPUT
PRINT SE (PICKRANDOM :QUALIFY)
_         (CHANGE.PERSON :USER.INPUT)
END
```

Now you can put both methods together. You can select between the methods at random, using the test **IF (RANDOM 2) = 0** to generate **TRUE** or **FALSE** with equal chances. You can also terminate the conversation if the user types **GOODBYE:**[6]

```
TO DOCTOR.LOOP
MAKE "USER.INPUT READLIST
IF :USER.INPUT = [GOODBYE]
_  [PRINT [COME SEE ME AGAIN] STOP]
```

---

[5] We use here the **PICKRANDOM** procedure (section 6.2). Notice that although we designed **PICKRANDOM** to pick a random word from a list of words, the generality of the Logo list operations **FIRST** and **BUTFIRST** ensures that the same procedure also works to pick a random element from any list.

[6] The conditional form **IFELSE** used in **DOCTOR.LOOP** is similar to **IF**, except that you specify both an action to perform if the test is true, and an alternative to perform if the test is false. The third line of **DOCTOR.LOOP** does either **HEDGE** or **RESPOND :USER.INPUT**, depending on whether **RANDOM 2** equals 0.

```
IFELSE (RANDOM 2) = 0
_ [HEDGE] [RESPOND :USER.INPUT]
DOCTOR.LOOP
END
```

All that is missing now is a procedure **DOCTOR** to start things going. This should initialize the lists **QUALIFY**, **HEDGES**, and **PRONOUNS** used above, print an opening remark, and call **DOCTOR.LOOP**:

```
TO DOCTOR
MAKE "QUALIFY
_ [[YOU SEEM TO THINK]
_ [YOU FEEL THAT]
_ [YOU SAY]]
MAKE "HEDGES
_ [[PLEASE GO ON]
_ [PLEASE CONTINUE]
_ [MANY PEOPLE HAVE THE SAME SORTS OF FEELINGS]]
MAKE "PRONOUNS [[I YOU] [ME YOU] [MY YOUR] [AM ARE]]
PRINT [WHAT SEEMS TO BE THE PROBLEM]
DOCTOR.LOOP
END
```

Extending the program

The previous program is only a simple sketch. One immediate extension you'll want to make is to increase its repertoire of **HEDGES** and **QUALIFY**, so that the responses are more varied. Another idea is to upgrade the **RESPOND** procedure not only to change first person words to second person, but also second person to first. For instance, if the user types

YOU ARE NOT BEING VERY HELPFUL TO ME

the program should respond with something like

YOU FEEL THAT I AM NOT BEING VERY HELPFUL TO YOU

Another idea is this. Every so often, the program should save away the user's response. Then, a few exchanges later, the program could say something like "Earlier you said that ..." Still other ideas are to have the program select special responses, when the user mentions certain words, like "computer."

By including more and more of these features, you can make the program's conversations quite elaborate. The responses of Weizenbaum's original **DOCTOR** program have been occasionally mistaken for those of a real person, and this has led some people to advocate using such programs in the treatment of psychiatric patients. Others, including Weizenbaum, maintain that this would be extremely unethical. For a further discussion of these points see Weizenbaum's book [31].

10.3.2. Example: The ANIMAL Program

ANIMAL is a well-known computer program that asks the user to think of an animal and then tries to guess what animal it is by asking yes-or-no questions. Here is a sample session with the program:

ANIMAL
THINK OF AN ANIMAL. I WILL
TRY TO GUESS IT BY ASKING QUESTIONS.
DOES IT HAVE LEGS?
YES

IS IT A CAT?
YES

LOOK HOW SMART I AM!
LET'S TRY AGAIN...
THINK OF AN ANIMAL. I WILL
TRY TO GUESS IT BY ASKING QUESTIONS.
DOES IT HAVE LEGS?
NO

DOES IT CRAWL?
YES
IS IT A SNAKE?
YES

LOOK HOW SMART I AM!
LET'S TRY AGAIN...

.

.

The cleverness of the program is that it learns from its mistakes. Here is what happens when it guesses incorrectly:

DOES IT HAVE LEGS?
NO

DOES IT CRAWL?
YES

IS IT A SNAKE?
NO

OH WELL, I WAS WRONG. WHAT WAS IT?
EARTHWORM
PLEASE TYPE IN A QUESTION WHOSE ANSWER
IS YES FOR AN EARTHWORM AND
NO FOR A SNAKE
DOES IT LIVE UNDERGROUND?
LET'S TRY AGAIN...

.

.

.

The next time the program runs across this situation it will behave like this:

DOES IT HAVE LEGS?
NO

DOES IT CRAWL?
YES

DOES IT LIVE UNDERGROUND?

.

.

So the program becomes smarter and smarter as it is used more and more.

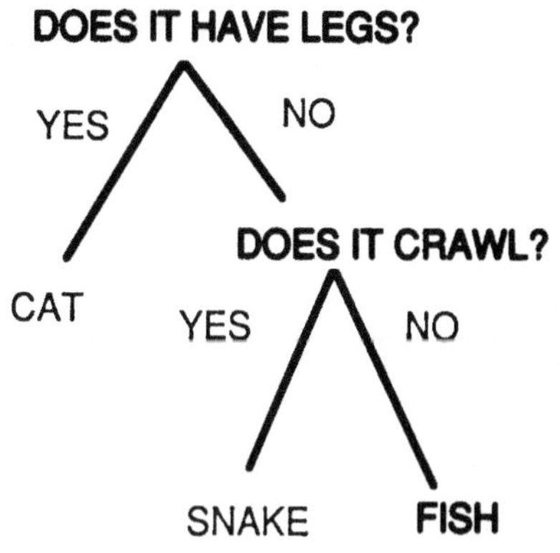

How the ANIMAL program works

The key to the program is its knowledge structure. This can be thought of as a tree, as shown in figure 10.2. The tree is made up of "nodes," where each node consists of a **QUESTION** to ask, a **YES.BRANCH** to follow if the answer to the question is yes, and a **NO.BRANCH** to follow if the answer is no.

The basic operation of the program is to begin at the top node of the tree and work its way down, following the **YES.BRANCH** or the **NO.BRANCH** according to the answer to the **QUESTION**. If the program reaches a node that consists of only a single item, it guesses that as the animal.

When the program guesses incorrectly, it "gets smarter" by expanding the tree. It asks the user for the correct response and a question that distinguishes the correct response from the incorrect response. It then replaces the old single-item node by a new node made up of the user's question, the correct response as the **YES.BRANCH** and the old incorrect response as the **NO.BRANCH**. For example, to learn the difference between a snake and an earthworm, the program expands the tree, replacing the **SNAKE** node by a node whose **QUESTION** is **DOES IT LIVE UNDERGROUND?**, whose **YES.BRANCH** is **EARTHWORM**, and whose **NO.BRANCH** is **SNAKE**.[7]

That's all there is to it.

Using lists

The **ANIMAL** program can be conveniently written in Logo, because lists are just the right tool for representing the knowledge tree. You can think of the tree as a list called **KNOWLEDGE** that has

DOES IT HAVE LEGS?

YES   NO

CAT

DOES IT CRAWL?

YES   NO

SNAKE   **FISH**

Figure 10.2: Knowledge tree for the **ANIMAL** program

---

[7] Of course, if the user types in *wrong* information, then the program will get stupider instead of smarter. Also, the program we shall describe below does not check for *inconsistent* responses on the part of the user. Extending the program to do so is a good project.

three elements: a **QUESTION**, a **YES.BRANCH**, and a **NO.BRANCH**. Of course **YES.BRANCH** and **NO.BRANCH** may themselves be lists that have the same structure. And so you have sublists and sublists, until you finally reach branches that are words, which give the actual animals to be guessed.

Here is a Logo list that represents the tree shown in figure 10.2:

```
[[DOES IT HAVE LEGS?]
 CAT
 [[DOES IT CRAWL?]
  SNAKE
  FISH]]
```

When snake is distinguished from earthworm, the list becomes

```
[[DOES IT HAVE LEGS?]
 CAT
 [[DOES IT CRAWL?]
  [[DOES IT LIVE UNDERGROUND?]
   EARTHWORM
   SNAKE]
  FISH]]
```

With the program's knowledge structured in this way, you can extract the **QUESTION**, **YES.BRANCH**, and **NO.BRANCH** parts of a given node by using the following procedures:

```
TO QUESTION :NODE
OUTPUT FIRST :NODE
END

TO YES.BRANCH :NODE
OUTPUT FIRST (BUTFIRST :NODE)
END

TO NO.BRANCH :NODE
OUTPUT LAST :NODE
END
```

The main procedure

Here is the procedure that starts the program:

```
TO ANIMAL
PRINT [THINK OF AN ANIMAL.  I WILL]
PRINT [TRY TO GUESS IT BY ASKING QUESTIONS]
CHOOSE.BRANCH :KNOWLEDGE
PRINT [LET'S TRY AGAIN...]
ANIMAL
END
```

It prints the instructions, does the guessing, and continues this over and over. The real work is done by the **CHOOSE.BRANCH** procedure, which is meant to be called with a node as input. It is initially called with the node that is the entire **KNOWLEDGE** list of the program:

```
TO CHOOSE.BRANCH :NODE
IF (WORDP :NODE) [GUESS :NODE STOP]
MAKE "RESPONSE
_  ASK.YES.OR.NO (QUESTION :NODE)
IFELSE :RESPONSE = [YES]
_  [CHOOSE.BRANCH (YES.BRANCH :NODE)]
_  [CHOOSE.BRANCH (NO.BRANCH :NODE)]
END
```

CHOOSE.BRANCH implements precisely the technique explained above. It asks the question associated with the node and then continues with the **YES.BRANCH** or the **NO.BRANCH** according to the result of the question. When it reaches a node that is a single word, it uses that as its guess. (The **GUESS** procedure, which actually makes the guess, is discussed below.) Notice how the "continues with ..." part of the strategy is implemented by a **CHOOSE.BRANCH** calling itself recursively using the appropriate branch as the new node.

Asking questions

The following procedure is used to ask a yes-or-no question. It takes the question as input and returns either **[YES]** or **[NO]**.

```
TO ASK.YES.OR.NO :QUESTION
PRINT :QUESTION
MAKE "INPUT READLIST
IF :INPUT = [YES] [OUTPUT [YES]]
IF :INPUT = [NO] [OUTPUT [NO]]
PRINT [PLEASE TYPE "YES" OR "NO" ]
OUTPUT ASK.YES.OR.NO :QUESTION
END
```

If the user responds with something other than **YES** or **NO**, the procedure repeats the question, using the same "try again" method as with the **READNUMBER** procedure of section 6.1.

"A" or "an"

One nicety that the program must handle when making guesses is to distinguish between animal names that begin with vowels and those that do not. So, if the guess is "snake" the program should ask "Is it *a* snake?" while, if the guess is "earthworm" the program should ask "Is it *an* earthworm?" The following procedure helps to do this. It takes a word as input and outputs a sentence consisting of the word preceded by "a" or "an" as appropriate. Compare this with the the **BEGINS.WITH.VOWEL?** procedure in section 5.6.

```
TO ADD.A.OR.AN :WORD
IFELSE MEMBERP (FIRST :WORD) [A E I O U]
_ [OUTPUT SENTENCE "AN :WORD]
_ [OUTPUT SENTENCE "A :WORD]
END
```

Making a guess

When **CHOOSE.BRANCH** reaches a node with only a single animal, it calls the **GUESS** procedure with that animal as input.

```
TO GUESS :ANIMAL
MAKE "FINAL.QUESTION
_ (SE [IS IT] (ADD.A.OR.AN :ANIMAL) [?])
MAKE "RESPONSE
_ ASK.YES.OR.NO :FINAL.QUESTION
IFELSE :RESPONSE = [YES]
_ [PRINT [LOOK HOW SMART I AM!]]
_ [GET.SMARTER :ANIMAL]
END
```

GUESS first formulates the appropriate "Is it (a or an) ... ?" question and gets the response. If the guess is correct, the program brags about how smart it is and stops, returning eventually to the **ANIMAL** procedure, which starts the next round. If the guess is wrong, the program must grow smarter.

Getting smarter

Getting smarter consists, first of all, of asking the user for the right animal and for a question that distinguishes the right animal from the wrong one. Observe how the "a or an" choice is needed to construct the request for a question.

```
TO GET.SMARTER :WRONG.ANSWER
PRINT [OH WELL, I WAS WRONG.  WHAT WAS IT?]
MAKE "RIGHT.ANSWER (LAST READLIST)
PRINT [PLEASE TYPE IN A QUESTION WHOSE ANSWER]
PRINT (SE [IS YES FOR]
_ (ADD.A.OR.AN :RIGHT.ANSWER) [AND])
PRINT (SE [NO FOR]
_ (ADD.A.OR.AN :WRONG.ANSWER))
MAKE "QUESTION READLIST
EXTEND.KNOWLEDGE
_ :QUESTION :RIGHT.ANSWER :WRONG.ANSWER
END
```

Once the new question and the two answers are in hand, the program proceeds to extend its knowledge. This is accomplished by resetting the list **KNOWLEDGE** to the result of starting with KNOWLEDGE and replacing the node consisting of just the old answer with a list formed from the question, the new animal as the **YES.BRANCH**, and the old answer as the **NO.BRANCH**.

```
TO EXTEND.KNOWLEDGE
_ :NEW.QUESTION YES.ANSWER :NO.ANSWER
MAKE "KNOWLEDGE
_   REPLACE :KNOWLEDGE
_       :NO.ANSWER
_       (LIST :NEW.QUESTION
_               :YES.ANSWER
_               :NO.ANSWER)
END
```

Finally, there is the procedure that does the actual replacement. This takes as inputs

- A list that represents a tree of **QUESTION—YES.BRANCH—NO.BRANCH** nodes

- A node to be replaced

- The thing to replace it with

The output of **REPLACE** is a copy of the tree with the old node replaced by the designated replacement.

```
TO REPLACE :TREE :NODE :REPLACEMENT
IF :TREE = :NODE [OUTPUT :REPLACEMENT]
IF WORDP :TREE [OUTPUT :TREE]
OUTPUT (LIST
_   QUESTION :TREE
_   REPLACE (YES.BRANCH :TREE)
_     :NODE
_     :REPLACEMENT
_   REPLACE (NO.BRANCH :TREE)
_     :NODE
_     :REPLACEMENT)
END
```

REPLACE is the most difficult procedure in the **ANIMAL** program. It uses a recursive strategy somewhat as in the **SUBST** procedure (section 10.1.2) but more complicated. The idea is that if the tree itself is the node to replace, you output the replacement. Otherwise, the new tree should be formed from the original tree's **QUESTION**, together with the result of performing the replacement recursively in the **YES.BRANCH** and the **NO.BRANCH**. This reduces the substitution to operations on smaller and smaller subtrees of the original. Finally, when you reduce to nodes that are individual words, you should output the words themselves.

Running the program

Figure 10.3 shows the structure of procedure calls for the entire **ANIMAL** program.

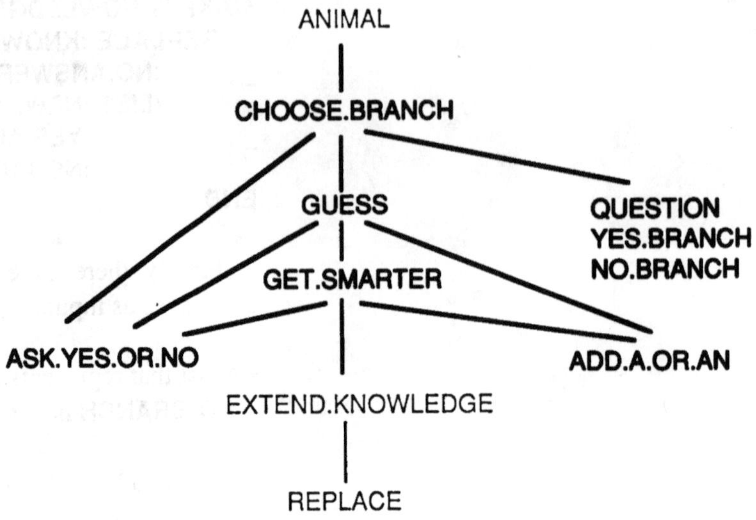

ANIMAL
|
CHOOSE.BRANCH

GUESS   **QUESTION**
      YES.BRANCH
GET.SMARTER   **NO.BRANCH**

ASK.YES.OR.NO   **ADD.A.OR.AN**

EXTEND.KNOWLEDGE
|
REPLACE

Figure 10.3: Structure of procedure calls in the **ANIMAL** program

To run the program, you initialize the **KNOWLEDGE** list to any animal you like, and run the **ANIMAL** procedure. For example,

MAKE "KNOWLEDGE "FISH
ANIMAL

When you are done with your session, you can save your workspace, which will include the final value of the **KNOWLEDGE** tree. Thus when you read the program in to play with it the next time, the wisdom gained during previous sessions will not be lost.

Modifications

ANIMAL is a lot of fun to use as it is, especially as you begin to input funny animals and outrageous questions. There are also many good projects that arise from extending the program's capabilities. One idea is to vary the responses that the program gives. Another is to have the program request not a literal yes-or-no question, but rather a fact that distinguishes between the two animals. Then the program can use this fact to generate its own question. This requires that you build in some knowledge about grammar, somewhat like the capabilities in the **DOCTOR** program. Finally—and this is really open-ended—you can try to make the program smart enough to distinguish legitimate responses from wisecracks. Here is a sample dialogue with a more sophisticated animal program:[8]

DOES IT HAVE HORNS?
YES
IS IT A BUFFALO?
NO

---

[8] The dialogue given here is with a program by B. Greenberg [14].

WELL, I'M NOT TOO SHARP TODAY. I GIVE UP.
JUST WHAT KIND OF BEAST DID YOU HAVE IN MIND?
A GAZELLE
 TELL ME SOMETHING ABOUT A GAZELLE
THAT IS NOT TRUE ABOUT A BUFFALO
A GAZELLE IS GRACEFUL
THAT WAS FUN. WANT TO TRY AGAIN?
MAYBE
HEY, CAN YOU GIVE ME A YES OR NO ANSWER
YES
DOES IT HAVE HORNS?
NO
IS IT A BUTTERFLY?
NO
WELL, I'M NOT TOO SHARP TODAY. I GIVE UP.
JUST WHAT KIND OF BEAST DID YOU HAVE IN MIND?
A PIG
TELL ME SOMETHING ABOUT A PIG THAT
IS NOT TRUE ABOUT A BUTTERFLY
A PIG IS SLOVENLY
THAT WAS FUN. WANT TO TRY AGAIN?
YES
DOES IT HAVE HORNS?
NO
IS THIS ANIMAL SLOVENLY?
YES
IS IT A PIG?
YES
HEY, HEY, I SURE AM CLEVER, HUH?
THAT WAS FUN. WANT TO TRY AGAIN?
YES
DOES IT HAVE HORNS
YES
IS THIS ANIMAL GRACEFUL?
YOU ARE NOT GRACEFUL
HEY CAN YOU GIVE ME A YES OR NO ANSWER?
NO
IS IT A BUFFALO?
NO
WELL, I'M NOT TOO SHARP TODAY. I GIVE UP.
JUST WHAT KIND OF BEAST DID YOU HAVE IN MIND?
BULL
TELL ME SOMETHING ABOUT A BULL
THAT IS NOT TRUE ABOUT A BUFFALO
**WHY DON'T YOU TELL ME SOMETHING,
YOU ELECTRONIC MORON?**
AW, BE SERIOUS. I ASKED YOU A REAL QUESTION
IT WOULD MARRY A COW

CHAPTER **11**

Glossary of Logo Primitive **Commands**

The complete Object Logo system is very extensive. It includes hundreds of built-in commands and predefined objects for manipulating text windows, graphics windows, menus, files, MIDI music, and robots. A complete description of all commands can be found in the Object Logo Reference Manual. This chapter lists the Object Logo primitive commands that are used in this book, together with a few other primitive commands that you will find useful for projects like the ones described in the preceding chapters.

11.1. Graphics Commands

BACK
Abbreviated **BK**
Example:

BACK 100
turtle moves backward 100 units

Takes one number as input and moves the turtle that many units in the direction opposite to that in which the turtle is facing. Draws a line if the pen is down.

BACKCOLOR
Outputs a number that describes the color of the Graphics window background. See **COLORVALUE.**

BACKPAT
Outputs a list of 8 numbers, as in **PENPATTERN,** that describes the background pattern of the Graphics window.

CLEAN
Takes no inputs. Clears the Graphics window. Does not change the turtle's position.

CLEARSCREEN
Abbreviated **CS**
Takes no input. Clears the graphics screen and homes and shows the turtle.

COLORVALUE
This command generates color numbers for use with **SETPENCOLOR** and **SETBACKCOLOR.** It takes as inputs three numbers each between 0 and 255. These numbers specify intensities of red, green, and blue. The output is an integer that encodes the corresponding color.

DOT   Example:

DOT [20 100]
a dot appears on the screen at a position (20, 100)

Takes as input a list specifying a screen position and places a dot (in the current pencolor) at that position. Does not move the turtle.

FORWARD   Abbreviated **FD**
Example:

FORWARD 100
turtle moves forward 100 units

Takes one numeric input. Moves the turtle the designated number of units in the direction in which it is facing. Draws a line if the pen is down.

HEADING   Example:

SETHEADING HEADING + 10
rotates the turtle 10 degrees clockwise

Takes no inputs. Outputs the turtle's heading as a number between 0 and 360.

HIDETURTLE   Abbreviated **HT**
Takes no inputs. Makes the turtle pointer disappear.

HOME   Takes no inputs. Moves the turtle to the center of the screen, pointing straight up.

LEFT   Abbreviated **LT**
Example:

LEFT 90
turtle rotates 90 degrees counterclockwise

Takes one numeric input. Rotates the turtle that many degrees counterclockwise.

PENCOLOR   Takes no inputs. Outputs a number representing the turtle's pen color. See **COLORVALUE**.

PENDOWN   Abbreviated **PD**
Takes no inputs. Causes the turtle to leave a trail when it moves.

PENERASE   Abbreviated **PE**
Takes no inputs. Causes the turtle to erase what it is drawing over.

PENMODE	Takes no inputs. Outputs the turtle's penmode, which is one of the following symbols: **UP, DOWN, ERASE, PAINT, REVERSE, DOWNNOT, ERASENOT, PAINTNOT, REVERSENOT.**
PENPATTERN	Outputs a list of 8 numbers, between 0 and 255, that describes the pattern drawn by the turtle's pen. The pattern is specified as pixels in an 8-by-8 grid. Each number encodes a row of in the grid: the eight 1-0 bits in the number's binary representation determine whether the corresponding eight pixels in the row are on or off.
PENREVERSE	Abbreviated **PX** Takes no inputs. Causes the turtle's pen to reverse what it is drawing over. (White becomes black, and black becomes white.)
PENUP	Abbreviated **PU** Takes no inputs. Causes the turtle to move without leaving a trail.
POSITION	Abbreviated **POS** Takes no inputs. Outputs the turtle's position as a list of x, y coordinates.
RIGHT	Abbreviated **RT** Example: **RIGHT 45** turtle rotates 45 degrees clockwise Takes one numeric input. Rotates the turtle that many degrees clockwise.
SETBACKCOLOR	Example: **SETBACKCOLOR 137** background color is now magenta Takes a numeric input that designates a color, and sets the background to that color. See **COLORVALUE**.
SETBACKPAT	Example: **SETBACKPAT [238 221 187 119 238 221 187 119]** background is now diagonally striped Takes list of 8 numbers that encodes a pattern, as in **PENPATTERN**, and sets the background pattern.
SETHEADING	Abbreviated **SETH** Example: **SETHEADING 180** turtle now faces straight down

Takes one numeric input. Rotates the turtle to point in the direction specified. The input is interpreted as a number in degrees. Zero is straight up, with heading increasing clockwise.

SETPENCOLOR   Example:

SETPENCOLOR 137
turtle now draws in magenta

Takes a numeric input that designates a color, and sets the turtle's pen color to that color. See **COLORVALUE.**

SETPENMODE   Takes as argument an symbol describing a pen mode (see **PENMODE** above) and sets the pen mode.

SETPOSITION   Abbreviated: **SETPOS**
Takes a list of two numbers (*x* and *y* coordinates) and moves the turtle to that position. Draws a line if the pen is down.

SETXCOR   Abbreviated: **SETX**
Takes one numeric input and moves the turtle horizontally to the specified *x*-coordinate. Draws a line if the pen is down.

SETYCOR   Abbreviated: **SETY**
Takes one numeric input and moves the turtle vertically to the specified *y*-coordinate. Draws a line if the pen is down.

SETXY   Example:

SETXY 100 50
turtle moves to position (100,50)

Takes two numeric inputs.   Moves the turtle to the specified point, where (0,0) is center of screen. Draws a line if the pen is down.

SHOWNP   Takes no inputs. Outputs **TRUE** if the turtle is currently being shown and **FALSE** if it isn't.

SHOWTURTLE   Abbreviated **ST**
Takes no inputs. Makes the turtle pointer appear.

TOWARDS   Example:

SETHEADING TOWARDS 100 50
turtle is now facing point (100,50)

Takes two numeric inputs. These are interpreted as the *x* and *y* coordinates of the point on the screen. **TOWARDS** outputs the heading from the turtle to the point.

XCOR Example:

SETX XCOR + 10
moves the turtle 10 units to the right

Takes no inputs. Outputs the turtle's *x* coordinate.

YCOR Takes no inputs. Outputs the turtle's *y* coordinate.

11.2. Numeric Operations

+ Example:

PRINT 5 + 2.5
7.5

Takes two numbers as inputs, and outputs their sum.

− Example:

PRINT 5 − 2
3
PRINT 1 + (−2)
−1

With two numeric inputs, outputs their difference. With one numeric input, outputs its negative.

* Example:

PRINT 5 * 2
10

Takes two numeric inputs, and outputs their product.

/ Example:

PRINT 5 / 2
5/2
PRINT 6 / 2
3
PRINT 6.34 / 2.78
2.280755

Outputs its first input divided by its second. If the inputs are integers or rational numbers, the result will also be either an integer or a rational number. Otherwise the result will be a real number.

∧   Example:

PRINT 13 ∧ 20
19004963774880799438801
PRINT 2.45 ∧ 17
4128796.0844
PRINT 17 ∧ 2.45
1034.18886

Outputs its first input raised to the power of its second input.

ABS   Takes one input and outputs the absolute value.

ARCSIN   Outputs the arc sine of its input, as an angle in degrees. The output is in the range $-90 \leq x < 90$.

ARCCOS   Outputs the arc cosine of its input as an angle in degrees. The output is in the range $0 \leq x < 180$.

ARCTAN   Outputs the arc tangent of its input, as an angle in degrees. The output is in the range $-90 \leq x < 90$.

COS   Outputs the cosine of its input as an angle in degrees.

DIFFERENCE   Example:

PRINT DIFFERENCE 37.5 6.8
30.7

Takes two inputs and outputs the result of subtracting the second input from the first.

EXP   Example:

PRINT EXP 3
20.0855369

Outputs *e* raised to the power of the input, where *e* is the base of the system of natural logarithms.

INTEGER   Example:

PRINT INTEGER 5.6
5
PRINT INTEGER (− 5.6)
−5

Takes one numeric input and converts it to an integer by truncating any fractional part.

INTQUOTIENT   Example:

PRINT INTQUOTIENT 129 6
21
PRINT INTQUOTIENT 129.999 6.999
21

Takes two inputs. Divides the integer part of the first input by the integer part of the second input and outputs the result, truncated to an integer.

LN   Outputs the natural logarithm of its input.

LOG   Example:

PRINT LOG 2048 2
11

Takes two inputs, *a* and *b*. Outputs the logarithm of *a* to the base *b*.

POWER   Takes two inputs and outputs the first input raised to the power of the second input. (**POWER** is a prefix form of ^.)

PRODUCT   Example:

PRINT (PRODUCT 1.3 47 98.5)
6018.35

Takes a variable number of inputs (default is 2) and outputs their product.

QUOTIENT   Example:

PRINT QUOTIENT 129.999 6.999
18.5739

Outputs the result of dividing the first input by the second input (contrast with **INTQUOTIENT**).

RANDOM   Takes one input *n*, and outputs a randomly chosen non-negative integer less than the integer part of *n*. When Logo is started, identical sequences of calls to **RANDOM** will yield repeatable sequences of random numbers.

REMAINDER   Example:

PRINT REMAINDER 35 10
5
PRINT 35 \ 10
5

Outputs the remainder of its first input modulo its second input. Backslash (\) is an infix form of **REMAINDER**.

RERANDOM   Takes no inputs. Resets the random number generator. Each time **RERANDOM** is run, subsequent calls to **RANDOM** will yield the same sequence of values.

ROUND   Outputs the nearest integer to its input. If the decimal part is .5, it rounds away from zero.

SIN   Outputs the sine of its input as an angle in degrees.

SQRT   Outputs the square root of its input.

SUM   Example:

PRINT (SUM 13 29 2)
44

Takes a variable number of inputs (default is 2) and outputs their sum.

11.3. Word and List Operations

BUTFIRST   Abbreviated **BF**
Example:

SHOW BUTFIRST [THIS IS A LIST]
[IS A LIST]
PRINT BUTFIRST "ABRACADABRA
BRACADABRA

If input is a list, outputs a list containing all but the first element. If input is a word, outputs a word containing all but the first character. Gives an error when called with the empty word or the empty list as input.

BUTLAST   Abbreviated **BL**
Example:

PRINT BUTLAST [THIS IS A LIST]
[THIS IS A]
PRINT BUTLAST "ABRACADABRA
ABRACADABR

If input is a list, outputs a list containing all but the last element. If input is a word, outputs a word containing all but the last character. Gives an error when called with the empty word or the empty list as input.

COUNT   Example:

PRINT COUNT [FEE FIE FOE FUM]
4
PRINT COUNT "ABCDE
5
PRINT COUNT [[THIS IS A] [NESTED LIST]]
2

If the input is a list, outputs the number of items in the list. If the input is a word, outputs the number of characters in the word.

FIRST   Example:

PRINT FIRST [THIS IS A LIST]
[THIS]
PRINT FIRST "ABRACADABRA
A

If input is a list, outputs the first element.   If input is a word, outputs the first character. Gives an error when called with the empty word or the empty list as input.

FPUT   Example:

PRINT FPUT [A B] [C D]
[A B] C D

The second input must be a list. Outputs a list consisting of the first input followed by the elements of the second input.

ITEM   Example:

PRINT ITEM 3 [FEE FIE FOE FUM]
FOE
PRINT ITEM 2 [[HOBBY HORSE] [PACK RAT] BANANA]
PACK RAT
PRINT ITEM 3 "CAT
T

Takes two inputs, a number and a word or list. The number is truncated to an integer n. If the second input is a list, outputs the nth element of the list. If the second input is a word, outputs the nth character of the word.

LAST   Example:

PRINT LAST [THIS IS A LIST]
LIST
PRINT LAST "ABRACADABRAX
X

If input is a list outputs the last element. If input is a word, outputs the last character. Gives an error when called with the empty word or the empty list as input.

LIST   Example:

PRINT LIST "A "B
A B
PRINT (LIST "A "B [1 2 3] "C)
A B [1 2 3] C

Takes a variable number of inputs (two by default) and outputs a list of the inputs.

LPUT   Example:

PRINT LPUT "Z [W X Y]
W X Y Z
PRINT LPUT [A B] [C D]
C D [A B]

Second input must be a list. Outputs a list consisting of the elements of the second input followed by the first input.

SENTENCE   Abbreviated **SE**
Example:

PRINT SENTENCE "HELLO "THERE
HELLO THERE
PRINT SENTENCE [THIS IS] [A LIST]
THIS IS A LIST
PRINT (SENTENCE "THIS [IS] [A LIST])
THIS IS A LIST
PRINT SENTENCE [[HERE IS] A] [NESTED LIST]
[HERE IS] A NESTED LIST

Takes a variable number of inputs. (The default is two.) If the inputs are all lists, combines all their elements into a single list. If any inputs are words, they are regarded as one-word lists in performing this operation.

WORD   Example:

PRINT WORD "MISH "MASH
MISHMASH
PRINT (WORD 123 45 678)
12345678

Takes a variable number of inputs (default is two). Outputs a word that is the concatenation of the characters of its inputs (which must be words).

11.4. Defining and Editing Procedures

TO and EDIT are the most commonly used operations for creating and changing procedures. Object Logo includes other operations that allow more advanced manipulation of procedure definitions.

DEFINE Example:

DEFINE "PTSUM [[:X :Y] [PRINT :X] [PRINT :X + :Y]]

defines the procedure

TO PTSUM :X :Y
PRINT :X
PRINT :X + :Y
END

Takes two inputs. First is a name, and second is a list whose elements are a list of inputs and a list for each line, and defines a procedure accordingly.   Note that you normally use TO rather than DEFINE in order to define procedures. DEFINE is useful for writing procedures that define other procedures, as in the extended INSTANT system described in section 10.2.2.

EDIT Example:

EDIT [SQUARE]
sets up procedure SQUARE for editing

Opens an editor window with the procedure set up for editing as shown in figure 1.12 Can also take auxiliary words NAMES and PROCEDURES, to edit all names or procedure definitions.

END Terminates a procedure definition.

TEXT Example:

TO PTSUM :X :Y
PRINT :X
PRINT :X + :Y
END

PRINT TEXT "PTSUM
[:X :Y][PRINT :X][PRINT :X + :Y]

Takes a procedure name as input and outputs procedure text as a list, whose format is as described under DEFINE.

TO Begins a procedure definition.

11.5. Conditional Expressions

Logo includes two basic facilities for allowing the user to write programs that perform tests and do different things depending on the outcomes. One is **IF** and **IFELSE**. The other is **TEST ... IFTRUE ... IFFALSE**, which is often simpler to use.

AND

Example:

PRINT (AND (1 + 1 = 2) (5 = 4) (1 = 1))
FALSE

Takes a variable number of inputs (default is two). Each input should be either **TRUE** or **FALSE**. Outputs **TRUE** if all are **TRUE**, otherwise outputs **FALSE**.

IF

Example:

IF :X=5 [STOP]

Used in the basic conditional form **IF** <condition> <action>. The condition is tested. If it is true, then the action is performed. Note that the action is enclosed in brackets.

IFELSE

Example:

IFELSE :X=5 [STOP] [TRYAGAIN]

Used in the conditional form **IFELSE** <condition> <action1> <action2>. The condition is tested. If it is true, <action1> is performed. If it is false, <action2> is performed.

IFFALSE

Evaluates its input only if result of preceding **TEST** was false. See **TEST**.

IFTRUE

Evaluates its input only if result of preceding **TEST** was true. See **TEST**.

NOT

Example:

IF NOT (:X = :Y) [PRINT "UNEQUAL]

Outputs **TRUE** if its input is **FALSE**, **FALSE** if its input is **TRUE**

OR

Example:

PRINT (OR (1 + 1 = 2) (5 = 4) (1 = 1))
TRUE

Takes variable number of inputs (default is two) and outputs TRUE if at least one is **TRUE**, otherwise outputs **FALSE**.

TEST   Example:

>   **TEST 12 = WORD 1 2**
>   **IFFALSE [PRINT "NO]**
>   **IFTRUE [PRINT "YES]**
>   YES

>   Tests a condition to be used in conjunction with **IFTRUE** and **IFFALSE**.

11.6. Predicates Used with Conditional Expressions

The conditional expressions of the previous section make use of predicates, or operations that output either **TRUE** or **FALSE**. A predicate can be any procedure that outputs the word **TRUE** or the word **FALSE**. Here are some built-in predicates:

>   Example:

>   **IF :X > :Y [STOP]**

>   Outputs **TRUE** if its first input is greater than its second, **FALSE** otherwise.

<   Outputs **TRUE** if its first input is less than its second, **FALSE** otherwise.

=   Example:

>   **PRINT 20 = WORD 2 0**
>   TRUE
>   **PRINT "A = [A]**
>   FALSE
>   **PRINT [A B] = SENTENCE "A "B**
>   TRUE

>   If both inputs are numbers, compares them to see if they are numerically equal. If both inputs are words, compares them to see if they are identical character strings. If both inputs are lists, compares them to see if their corresponding elements are equal. Outputs **TRUE** or **FALSE** accordingly.

EMPTYP   Example:

>   **PRINT EMPTYP BUTFIRST [LOLLIPOP]**
>   TRUE
>   **PRINT EMPTYP BUTFIRST "X**
>   TRUE

>   Takes one input. Outputs **TRUE** if the input is the empty word or the empty list, **FALSE** otherwise.

EQUALP	This is a prefix form of **=**.
LISTP	Outputs **TRUE** if its input is a list, **FALSE** otherwise.
MEMBERP	Example:

PRINT MEMBERP "A [ONCE UPON A TIME]
TRUE
PRINT MEMBERP [A B] [[A B] [C D]]
TRUE
PRINT MEMBERP "M "TIME
TRUE

Takes an item and a list, or a character and a word as inputs. Outputs **TRUE** if the item is a member of the list, or if the character is one of the characters in the word, **FALSE** otherwise.

NUMBERP	Outputs **TRUE** if its input is a number, **FALSE** otherwise.
WORDP	Outputs **TRUE** if its input is a word, **FALSE** otherwise.

11.7. Controlling Procedure Evaluation

OUTPUT	Abbreviated **OP**

Takes one input. Causes the current procedure to stop and output the result to the calling procedure.

REPEAT	Example:

REPEAT 3 [PRINT "HELLO]
HELLO
HELLO
HELLO

Takes a number and a list as input. **RUN**s the list the designated number of times. If the number is not an integer it is first truncated to an integer.

RUN	Example:

MAKE "X [PRINT]
RUN SENTENCE :X 5
5

Takes a list as input. Evaluates the list as if it were a typed in command line.

STOP	Causes the current procedure to stop and return control to the calling procedure.

TOPLEVEL   Stops the current procedure and all calling procedures and returns control to top level. Note the difference between **TOPLEVEL** and **STOP**. **STOP** stops the current procedure only and continues evaluation with the calling procedure, whereas **TOPLEVEL** stops evaluation of the whole program.

11.8. Input and Output

ASCII   Takes a character as input and outputs the number that is the ASCII code of that character.

CHAR   Takes an integer as input and outputs the character whose ASCII code is that integer.

CLEARTEXT   Takes no inputs. Clears the Listener window.

CLEARINPUT   Takes no inputs. Clears any pending keyboard input.

KEYP   Takes no inputs. Outputs **TRUE** if a keyboard character is pending, otherwise outputs **FALSE**.

PRINT   Abbreviated **PR**
Example:

```
PRINT "HI
HI
(PRINT "HELLO "OUT "THERE )
HELLO OUT THERE
PRINT [HELLO OUT THERE]
HELLO OUT THERE
```

Takes a variable number of inputs (default is 1). Prints them on the screen, separated by spaces, and moves cursor to the next line. When **PRINT** prints lists, the outermost pair of brackets is not printed.

READCHAR   Abbreviated **RC**
Takes no inputs. Outputs the least recent character in the character buffer, or if empty, waits for an input character.

READLIST   Abbreviated **RL**
Takes no inputs. Waits for an input line to be typed, terminated with RETURN. Outputs the line (as a list).

READWORD   Abbreviated **RW**
Takes no inputs. Waits for an input line to be typed, terminated with RETURN. Outputs the line (as a word).

SHOW   Like **PRINT**, except that is prints the outer brackets around lists. For example

PRINT [HI]
HI
SHOW [HI]
[HI]
PRINT "HI
HI
SHOW "HI
HI

TYPE   Like **PRINT**, but does not move cursor to the next line after printing. With multiple inputs, does not print spaces between the inputs.

WAIT   Takes a number as input and waits for that many seconds. The number need not be an integer.

11.9. Naming

LOCAL   Normally, variable names that are declared as inputs are *local* to the procedure in which they are declared, while other variable names are not. The **LOCAL** command allows you to declare other names besides inputs to be local to a given procedure. See section 5.5.1 for an explanation of local and global variables.

MAKE   Example:

MAKE "APPLE 50
PRINT :APPLE
50

Takes two inputs, the first of which must be a word. Assigns the second input to be the value associated with the first input.

NAME   This is equivalent to **MAKE** with the inputs reversed.
Example:

NAME [BATMAN SUPERMAN BOGEYMAN] "SUPERHEROES
PRINT :SUPERHEROES
BATMAN SUPERMAN BOGEYMAN

NAMEP   Outputs **TRUE** if its input has a value associated with it.

PUBLIC   Declares a variable to be public. A procedure's public variables in a procedure can be accessed by all the procedures that it calls. See section 5.5.2 for an explanation.

THING   Example:

MAKE "APPLE 50
PRINT THING "APPLE
50

Outputs the value of its input (which must be a word). **THING "XXX** is normally abbreviated as **:XXX**.

11.10. Objects

ASK   Example:

ASK :SEBASTIAN [FORWARD 25]

Take two inputs, an object and a list of commands. Causes that object to do the commands.

EXIST   Example:

ASK :SEBASTIAN [EXIST]

Initializes a new object.

KINDOF   Example:

MAKE "SEBASTIAN KINDOF TURTLE

Takes a variable number of inputs (the default is 1). Each input is an object. Makes an object a that inherits from all of these other objects.

ONEOF   Example:

MAKE "SEBASTIAN ONEOF TURTLE

Takes a variable number of inputs (the default is 1). Each input is an object. Makes an object a that inherits from all of these other objects. **KINDOF** and **ONEOF** are almost the same, except that **ONEOF** automatically asks the new object to **EXIST**.

SOMETHING   Example:

MAKE "AMANDA SOMETHING

Outputs a prototype object that has no pre-defined behavior.

TALKTO   Example:

TALKTO :AMANDA

Takes an object as input. After issuing **TALKTO** all subsequent top-level commands will be run in the specified object.

USUAL	Example: **ASK :SLOWTURTLE [TO FORWARD :DIST]** **REPEAT :DIST [USUAL.FORWARD 1]** **END** **USUAL** is a prefix that is preprended to the name of a procedure within the definition of another procedure with the same name. This tells Object Logo to use the procedure definition from a parent object. See section 7.3.2 for an explanation.

11.11. Filing and Managing Workspace

BURYNAME	Like **BURYPROC** but applies to names of variables rather than to procedure names.
BURYPROC	Takes a procedure name, or a list of procedure names, and hides the procedures, so they will not be affected by save, printout, and erase commands.
ERASE	Abbreviated **ER** Example: **ERASE [SQUARE]** gets rid of the procedure **SQUARE** Takes a procedure name or a list of procedure names. Erases designated procedures from workspace.
ERASEALL	Abbreviated **ERALL** Erases all procedures and variables from the workspace.
ERASENAME	Abbreviated **ERN** Takes a variable name, or a list of variable names, and erases the variables from the workspace.
ERNS	Erases all variables from the workspace.
ERPS	Erases all procedures from the workspace.
GOODBYE	Takes no inputs. Clears workspace and shuts down Logo.
LOAD	Example: **LOAD "MYFILE** Reads a file from disk. Takes file name as input.
POALL	Prints the names and values of all variables, and all procedure definitions.

PONS	Prints the names and values of all variables.
POPS	Prints the definitions of all procedures.
POTS	Prints the titles of all procedures.
PRINTOUT	Abbreviated **PO** Takes a procedure name, or a list of procedure names, and prints the definitions of the procedures.
SAVE	Example: **SAVE "MYFILE** Saves the contents of the workspace on disk. Takes file name as input.
UNBURYNAME	Like **UNBURYPROC** but applies to names of variables rather than to procedure names.
UNBURYPROC	Takes a procedure name, or a list of procedure names, and unburies the procedures.

11.12. Debugging Aids

CONTINUE	Abbreviated **CO** Takes no inputs. Resumes evaluation after a **PAUSE**.
DEBUG	Takes no inputs. Causes Logo to **PAUSE** when there is an error.
NODEBUG	Causes Logo to leave **DEBUG** mode.
PAUSE	Takes no inputs. Stops evaluation and allows command lines to be evaluated in the current local environment. Evaluation can be resumed with **CONTINUE**. Equivalent to the interrupt character **Command-Comma**.
STEP	Takes a procedure name, or a list of procedure names as input. Causes Logo to stop before each line of the procedure is run, and wait for the user to type a character.
TRACE	Takes a procedure name, or a list of procedure names as input. Causes Logo to print information about the inputs and outputs whenever the procedure runs.
UNSTEP	Takes a procedure name, or a list of procedure names as input. Turns off stepping for the indicated procedure.
UNTRACE	Takes a procedure name, or a list of procedure names as input. Turns off tracing for the indicated procedure.

WATCH	Takes a variable name, or a list of variable names. as input. Causes Logo to display a window that shows the value of the variable and is updated whenever the value changes.
UNWATCH	Takes a variable name, or a list of variable names. as input. Turns off watching for the indicated variable.

11.13. Primitives for Handling Properties

Properties are a built-in feature that Object Logo provides for arranging information in associative tables. See section 10.1.2.

GETPROP	Takes as inputs a symbol and a property name. Returns the value of the associated property for that symbol, or the empty list if there is no such property.
PLIST	Takes a symbol as input and returns that symbol's properties, in list form.
POPLS	Prints the names and property lists of all symbols that have property lists.
PUTPROP	Takes a symbol, a property, and a value as inputs. Associates that property value to the symbol. Example:

```
PUTPROP "BASIC "POWER "LIMITED
PUTPROP "BASIC "SIZE "SMALL
GETPROP "BASIC "POWER
LIMITED
PRINT PLIST "BASIC
SIZE SMALL POWER LIMITED
```

REMPROP	Takes a symbol and a property name as inputs and removes the corresponding property from the symbol.

11.14. Command Keys

The following command keys work at all times:

Command-Period	Interrupt the current procedure and return to top level
Command-Comma	Pause the current procedure
Command-Q	Quit
Command-S	Ask top window to WSave
Command-1	Activates the Listener window
Command-2	Activates the Graphics window
Command-3	Activates the File window

The following command keys work in all text windows:

Command-A	select All text in the top window
Command-B	Move Back one character
Command-C	Copy selection to clipboard
Command-D	Delete next character after the selection
Command-F	Move Forward one character
Command-N	Move to Next line
Command-P	Move to Previous line
Command-R	Run selection if any, otherwise run contiguous lines if insertion point is in a non-empty line, otherwise run entire contents of top window (except Listener)
Command-V	Paste contents of clipboard into window
Command-X	Delete selection and copy to clipboard
Tab	Start a continuation line by inserting **Return, underscore, space**
Enter	Run selection or current line directing output to current window

The following command keys work in history area of Listener windows:

Return, or Enter	Copy selection or current boldface part of line to end of input area
Command-R	Copy selection to end and Run it, or copy current line to end and Run it
Command-Option-C	Copy boldface characters of selection to clipboard
Command-Option-X	Delete selection and copy boldface characters to clipboard

The following command keys work in the input area of Listener windows:

Return, or Enter	Run entire input area
Shift-Return	Continue input on a new line
Command-Return	Ignore current input and type a new prompt
Command-X	If no selection, delete the entire input area and copy to clipboard

The following command key works in Editor windows:

Command-R	Run selection, or Run entire window contents and close window

11.15. Error Messages

When Logo encounters an error, it signals that fact by halting program evaluation and printing a message of the form:

{message}, in {procedure}

For example:

You haven't told me how to FORWAXD, in BOX

In general, {message} is a description of the error and {procedure} is the name of the procedure that Logo was running when the error occurred.

This section lists a few of the most common the error messages encountered when using Object Logo and describes the conditions that commonly cause them.

You haven't told me how to {something}

This happens when Logo does not recognize the name of the procedure you are trying to run. Common causes are that you forgot to define the procedure in question, or that you used the wrong name. Typing errors also commonly cause this. For example, if you type **FORWAXD 100** instead of **FORWARD 100**, you will get the error You haven't told me how to FORWAXD.

{something} has no value.

This happens when you refer to the value of a name, but there is no such name in the environment. The causes are similar to those for the "I don't know how to" error message. Another cause is confusion between the *local* variables in a procedure and the global variables. For example, defining and running the procedure

TO INC :X
OUTPUT :X + 1
END

creates a variable X that is local to **INC**, but this does not mean that there is a global variable named **X**.

Not enough inputs to {something}

A procedure was called with too few inputs

{primitive} doesn't like {data} as input

happens when you try to use an operation with a kind of data that it cannot handle. For example,

PRINT 1 + "X

results in + doesn't like X as input.

References

A great deal has been written on Logo. A bibliography compiled at MIT in 1985 listed nearly 200 books and 800 papers on Logo and on learning with Logo. The following references show only a tiny sample of what is available. They include some of the early, seminal writings on Logo as well as some recent books on Logo programming and projects.

1. Abelson, H. and diSessa, A. *Turtle Geometry: The Computer as a Medium for Exploring Mathematics*. MIT Press, Cambridge, MA., 1981.

2. Allan, B. *Introducing Logo*. London: Granada Publishing, 1984.

3. Allen, J. R., Davis, E. R., and Johnson, J. F. *Thinking about TLC Logo, A Graphic Look at Computing with Ideas*. Holt, Rinehart and Winston, New York, 1984.

4. Bamberger, J. "Logo Music Projects: Experiments in Musical Perception and Design." MIT Artificial Intelligence Laboratory Memo no. 523, Cambridge, MA, 1979.

5. Bearden, D. *1, 2, 3, My Computer and Me: A Logo Funbook for Kids*. Prentice Hall, New York, 1983.

6. Boecker, H.-D., Eden, H., and Fischer, G. *Interactive Problem Solving Using LOGO*. Lawrence Erlbaum Associates, Hillsdale, New Jersey, 1991.

7. Clayson, J. *Visual Modeling with Logo: A Structural Approach to Seeing*. MIT Press, Cambridge, MA, 1988.

8. Cuoco, A. *Investigations in Algebra*. MIT Press, Cambridge, MA, 1990.

9. diSessa, A. "Unlearning Aristotelian Physics: A Study of Knowledge-Based Learning." Cognitive Science, vol. 6, pp. 37–75, 1982.

10. Feurzeig, W., Papert, S., Bloom, M., Grant, R., and Solomon, C. "Programming Languages as a Conceptual Framework for Teaching Mathematics." Bolt, Beranek and Newman, Inc., Report no. 1889, November, Cambridge, MA, 1969.

11. Friendly, M. *Advanced Logo, A Language for Learning.* Lawrence Erlbaum Associates, Hillsdale, New Jersey, 1988.

12. Goldenberg, E. P. *Special Technology for Special Children.* University Park Press, Baltimore, 1979.

13. Goldenberg, E. P. and Feurzeig, W. *Exploring Language with Logo.* MIT Press, Cambridge, MA, 1987.

14. Greenberg, B. *Notes on the Programming Language Lisp.* MIT Student Information Processing Board, Cambridge, MA, 1978.

15. Harvey, B. *Computer Science Logo Style.* In 3 volumes. MIT Press, Cambridge, MA, Vol. 1: 1985; vol. 2: 1986; vol. 3: 1987.

16. Hoyles, C., and Noss, R. (ed.). *Learning Mathematics and Logo.* MIT Press, Cambridge, MA, 1992.

17. Lawler, R. *Computer Experience and Cognitive Development.* Ellis Horwood, Chichester, England, 1985.

18. Lewis, P. *Approaching Precalculus Mathematics Discretely.* MIT Press, Cambridge, MA, 1990.

19. McDougall A., Adams, T., and Adams, P. *Learning Logo on the Apple II.* Prentice Hall, Sydney, Australia, 1982.

20. Nevile, L., and Dowling, C. *Let's Talk Apple Turtle.* Prentice Hall International, 1983.

21. Papert, S. *Mindstorms: Children, Computers, and Powerful Ideas.* Basic Books, New York, 1980.

22. Papert, S., diSessa, A., Watt, D., and Weir, S. "Final Technical Report to the National Science Foundation: Documentation and Assessment of a Children's Computer Laboratory." MIT Logo Project Memo. 52, Cambridge, MA, 1980.

23. Papert, S., and Solomon, C. "NIM: A Game-Playing Program." MIT Artificial Intelligence Laboratory Memo no. 254, Cambridge, MA, 1970.

24. Ross, P. M. *Logo Programming.* Addison-Wesley, London, 1983.

25. Soloway, E., and Spohrer, J. C. (editors). *Studying the Novice Programmer.* Lawrence Erlbaum Associates, Hillsdale, New Jersey, 1989.

26. Thornburg, D. D. *Discovering Apple Logo: An Invitation to the Art and Pattern of Nature.* Addison Wesley, London, 1983.

27. Thornburg, D. D. *Beyond Turtle Graphics, Further Explorations of Logo.* Addison Wesley, London, 1986.

28. Turkle, S. *The Second Self: Computers and the Human Spirit.* Granada, 1984.

29. Watt, D. *Learning with Logo.* McGraw Hill, UK. 1983.

30. Weir , S. *Untrapping Intelligence: Logo and Special Learning.* Harper and Row, New York, 1985.

31. Weizenbaum, J. *Computer Power and Human Reason.* W.A. Freeman & Co., San Francisco, 1976.

32. Winston, P., and Horn, B. *Lisp*, 3rd edition. Addison-Wesley, Reading, MA, 1989.

33. Yazdani, M. (editor). *New horizons in Educational Computing.* Wiley, 1984.

Index